Hopewell Furnace

A Guide to
Hopewell Furnace National Historic Site
Pennsylvania

Produced by the
Division of Publications
National Park Service

U.S. Department of the Interior
Washington, D.C. 1983

D1248716

About This Book

Hopewell Furnace, in Berks County, Pennsylvania, is typical of the ironmaking communities that flourished in 18th- and 19th-century America, setting the stage for this nation's later industrial progress. Hopewell's cold-blast, charcoal furnace produced pig iron and castings from 1771 until its last campaign in 1883—a span of service that made it one of Pennsylvania's important furnace operations. Today's traveler who spends a few hours exploring at Hopewell will experience the closest approximation we have of life at a 19th-century iron furnace. This book provides the historical and technological background for that setting. Part 1 is an overview of the early ironmaking industry by W. David Lewis, Hudson Professor of History and Engineering at Auburn University. Part 2, by Walter Hugins, Professor of History at the State University of New York at Binghamton, recounts the history of Hopewell's operation and the workers who kept it going. Part 3 is a guide to the main points of interest at Hopewell Furnace.

Library of Congress Cataloging in Publication Data
Hopewell Furnace, Hopewell Furnace National Historic Site, Pennsylvania.
(National Park Handbook; 124)
Supt. of Docs. no.: I29.9/5:124
1. Hopewell Furnace National Historic Site (Pa.)
2. Iron industry and trade—Pennsylvania—History
I. Lewis, W. David (Walter David), 1931-   . II. Hugins, Walter Edward, 1925-   . III. United States. National Park Service. Division of Publications. IV. Series: Handbook (United States. National Park Service. Division of Publications); 124.
TS229.5.U6H66   1983   974.8'16   83-600130
ISBN 0-912627-18-2

For sale by the Superintendent of Documents, U.S. Government Printing Office, Washington, DC 20402.
☆GPO:1983—381-611/303 Reprint 1988

Part 1

Ironmaking in Early America

The Iron Plantations

In the task of throwing light on our industrial history—or any other facet of the past—words alone cannot convey the complex reality of events that shaped our world. Pictures and even artifacts, removed from their original context, are unequal to the task. A well-restored historical scene will provide an intimate perspective on the world sketched by word and image, and for the truly receptive, kindle an imaginative empathy with the past. One such place is Hopewell Furnace National Historic Site, where a succession of energetic ironmasters, furnace workers, and other community members helped lay the foundations of American ironmaking technology.

Their precursors were the European settlers of the American wilderness who brought with them techniques for making tools and other objects from metals, particularly iron. Iron is one of the most abundant elements in the Earth's crust. Learning to exploit it, in the Middle East about 1500 years before Christ, was one of the great human achievements. The earliest method of ironmaking, which persisted for 3,000 years, involved the heating of iron ore in a charcoal fire. The ore was not actually melted, but with the help of a crude bellows was reduced to a spongy mass, called a "bloom." The impurities in the iron were expelled by repeated heating and hammering. This basic technology, requiring only rudimentary equipment, was sufficient to supply small quantities to blacksmiths. It was practiced extensively in colonial America in bloomeries along the Atlantic Seaboard, especially in Massachusetts, New Jersey, and Pennsylvania.

A few centuries before the American colonies were settled, a new type of ironworks had been developed in Europe which could smelt iron ore and produce much more of this vital material than a bloomery could. This was the blast furnace, a tall stone structure shaped like a flattened pyramid. In the blast process a "flux," usually limestone, was added to the ore and charcoal to promote the separation of impurities from the iron. This method was called "indirect" because, when the molten iron wasn't immediately cast into a product, crude bars ("pig iron") were cast which would then be worked in a refinery forge, or "finery," to produce a bar iron similar to that made directly from ore in the bloomery. This "wrought iron" could then be forged into many shapes, or sent through a rolling or slitting mill to produce plates, bars, or nail rods. Finally, through the "cementation" process, a bar of wrought iron could be converted to steel for use in swords, cutlery, or springs. With the introduction of blast furnace technology into America in the mid-17th century, colonial ironmasters began to turn out a broad range of iron products.

Rapid expansion of the colonial iron industry in the early 18th century was one of the early causes of conflict with England. That country's mercantilist philosophy of keeping its colonies in a state of economic dependence led to passage by Parliament in 1750 of a law prohibiting the building of any further colonial ironworks for the making of plates, nail rods, or steel. This essentially limited the American iron industry to the production of the most basic materials, such as pig iron, which could then be converted into profitable specialized products in the mother country. Colonial ironmasters scoffed at these restrictive efforts, however, and by the outbreak of the Revolution, the American iron industry accounted for about one-seventh of the world's output of pig iron, wrought iron, and castings.

Colonial iron production had begun slowly. An early attempt to establish an ironworks in Virginia was thwarted by an Indian attack in 1622. Another pioneering venture in Massachusetts—the construction of a blast furnace, a finery, and a slitting mill at a site known as Hammersmith on the Saugus River—ended in bankruptcy about 1670. From these unpromising origins, however, the industry took root and flourished. By the time of the Revolution, New England was dotted with ironworks. Massachusetts alone had at least 14 blast furnaces, 41 forges, several plate and rod mills, and a steel furnace.

New York's prerevolutionary iron industry included wealthy landowner Philip Livingston's well-known furnace and finery at Ancram in the Hudson Valley, and Peter Townsend's important Sterling Works in the Ramapo Mountains, which became famous for producing the massive iron chain that was strung across the Hudson at West Point to block the passage of British ships during the Revolution. In New Jersey, which possessed an abundance of iron ore in its northern mountains and southern bogs, the iron industry began to spread in the mid-18th century. Vast enterprises were attempted by such men as German-born entrepreneur Peter Hasenclever, who imported more than 500 skilled workers from Europe to build for British investors an extensive series of blast furnaces and fineries.

Among the Southern colonies, Maryland and Virginia developed significant ironworks, including the celebrated Principio facility, established shortly before 1720 at the head of the Chesapeake Bay by a group of English merchants. Limited ore supplies in the area of the furnace led to a partnership with George Washington's father, Augustine Washington, who owned valuable ore deposits along the Rappahannock River in Virginia. The Washingtons remained affiliated with Principio for many years.

Pennsylvania was by far the most important iron manufacturing colony. It possessed rich resources of ore and limestone as well as numerous rushing streams that provided waterpower for the furnaces and other ironworks that spread in every direction from Philadelphia, especially in the Schuylkill and Susquehanna River valleys. Pennsylvania's heritage of religious toleration also attracted many enterprising citizens who became active in the iron industry.

Although William Penn's early efforts to establish an ironmaking company in 1682 came to nothing, by 1716 Thomas Rutter had built the first bloomery forge in Pennsylvania near what is now Pottstown. In 1720 he built Colebrookdale, the first blast furnace in the colony. Other ironmasters soon followed, buying up huge acreages to provide the charcoal consumed by their furnaces. Samuel Nutt, whose bloomery near Coventry grew into the famous Coventry Iron Works, built in 1732 the first steel furnace in Pennsylvania. By 1770, when Mark Bird chose Berks County as the site for Hopewell Furnace, the area was already becoming a center of American industry. By this time ironmakers were expanding westward beyond the Susquehanna River, establishing ironworks in the Cumberland and Juniata Valleys. At least 21 blast furnaces, 45 forges, four bloomeries, six steel furnaces, three slitting mills, two plate mills, and one wire mill were built in the colony

between 1716 and 1776, with names like Reading, Warwick, Mount Pleasant, Durham, Cornwall, Elizabeth, Windsor, Rebecca, Pine Grove, and Mary Ann. Though the western operations were generally much smaller in acreage than the huge "iron plantations" in the east, many of the furnaces in both regions were owned by families— Ege, Potts, Grubb, Rutter, and Ross— who took pride in the craft and passed it along to succeeding generations. By 1800, most Pennsylvania ironmasters were native-born.

These iron plantations were built on very different social and economic foundations from those of their southern agricultural counterparts, but there were parallels in their size, rural setting, and concentration on one product. There was usually a spacious, richly furnished "Big House," surrounded by thousands of acres of woodland. The ironmaster who resided there often emulated the style of the English gentry, complete with elegant carriages and a pack of hunting hounds. He was at the pinnacle of an essentially self-contained, rural society that often numbered over 100 people, all of whose work was directly or indirectly related to the production of iron.

Many of these people lived in tenant houses furnished by the company. Much of their food was grown on acreage belonging to the company. They bought everything they couldn't grow or make themselves from the company store or itinerant peddlers. The heart of the community was the glowing furnace, whose cycles of filling and tapping set the pace of life. Some plantations met the furnace's endless demand for ore from their own mines, and then converted the raw iron into marketable products at their own forges.

These plantations proved an efficient response to the natural conditions imposed on ironmakers in the New World. But even while the young American charcoal iron industry was expanding, changes in the basic technology were occurring in Great Britain which would transform iron and steel manufacturing throughout the world. The most important of these changes, stimulated by a shortage of forest land in England, was Abraham Darby's substitution, in the early 18th century, of coke, a purified form of coal, for charcoal as a blast furnace fuel. The less fragile coke allowed taller furnaces and increased production, but North American ironmasters, because of the shortage of usable coal on the Atlantic seaboard and the seemingly endless forests, continued their dependence on charcoal well into the 19th century. "Blowing tubs," patented in 1762, gradually replaced the unsteady blast produced by the less efficient bellows. In 1785, Henry Cort developed his "puddling" process, in which pig iron was melted in a reverberatory furnace and stirred, or puddled, into a ball of malleable iron. This could immediately be passed through rollers without preliminary hammering, saving considerable time. Because the coal in a puddling furnace never touched the iron, and so could not contaminate it, a cheaper grade of fuel could be used.

While English ironmaking rode these breakthroughs to new levels of efficiency and productivity, American ironmasters remained tied to 18th-century technology until further developments forced them to adapt. Most important was "hot blast" iron smelting, developed in Scotland in 1828, in which the air blown into the furnace was preheated. A hot blast furnace produced more iron with less fuel. In Eastern Pennsylvania, hot blast furnaces

were constructed to burn the available anthracite coal. Ironmasters west of the Appalachians began to use bituminous coal extensively by the middle of the 19th century.

In the two decades preceding the Civil War, American ironmaking technology began to catch up with British practice. By the last quarter of the century the United States had become the world's foremost industrial nation, producing iron and steel in undreamed of quantities. Bessemer's conversion process, permitting the production of relatively inexpensive steel, revolutionized the market for pig iron, which now went into the production of steel for rails, bridges, structural supports for buildings, and a growing number of other uses. The enormous demand for iron and steel resulted in the centralization of the industry in such urban centers as Pittsburgh, Chicago, and the Birmingham-Chattanooga complex. The day of the small charcoal-fired blast furnace with its wooden water wheel had come to an end, though many charcoal furnaces such as Hopewell struggled on for a time.

The purpose of this handbook is to help us remember, to bring to light the persons and processes that for more than a century made Hopewell hum as it went about the making of iron and iron products. With the historical background provided in this section, the reader is better prepared for the story of Hopewell, as told in Section 2 by historian Walter Hugins. His narrative will extend and deepen one's visit to Hopewell, or, for those far removed, serve as the next best thing to being there. *W. David Lewis*

To 18th- and 19th-century Americans, truncated pyramids of stone were a familiar feature of the eastern landscape. These blast furnaces, 25 to 35 feet high, were always located at the base of a natural or constructed "furnace bank" to allow charging of the furnace from the top.

Across an elevated walkway, fillers rolled carts and barrows of iron ore, charcoal, and limestone from storage areas on the furnace bank. Every furnace was flanked with a large wooden water wheel turning in a pit. The wheel drove a pair of bellows, furnishing the air blast necessary to intensify the heat to smelting temperatures. A system of counterweights returned the bellows to their original position. By the late 18th century, bellows were rapidly being replaced by "blowing tubs," two large cylindrical casks in which air was alternately compressed by pistons driven by the wheel. This provided a more uniform blast than the bellows. In front of the furnace was the cast arch, where the molten iron was periodically tapped. The iron was run into ladles and then poured into flasks to produce finished products. Pig iron was made by running the molten iron into troughs dug in the sand floor of the cast house. Slag, the waste product of the smelting process, was disposed of at heaps, or crushed in stamping mills to retrieve residual iron.

Resources Vital to the Blast Furnace

Iron Ore
Iron oxides such as magnetite, limonite, red hematite, brown hematite, and carbonate were widely distributed in the American colonies. Outcroppings and deposits close to the surface were worked, although some shaft mining was done in the 18th century. Hopewell Furnace used magnetite ore, which was frequently 50 percent iron.

Limestone
Effective separation of iron from impurities in the ore required the addition of a "flux" to the furnace charge. This was normally limestone, though other materials, such as oyster shells, could be used. Ash produced by the charcoal fuels also served as a flux. Approximately 30 to 40 pounds of limestone were fed into the furnace for every 400 to 500 pounds of iron ore, depending on the purity of the latter.

Charcoal
Charcoal, an almost pure carbon fuel that burns with intense heat, was produced by the slow combustion of wood under carefully controlled conditions. Because large quantities of charcoal were used in smelting, blast furnaces were built on large tracts of woodland. The abundant American forests allowed ironmasters to use charcoal long after Europeans had converted to coal or coke.

Water Power

To provide power for the blast machinery, charcoal iron furnaces were built near rushing streams or dammed lakes. Water was diverted to the water wheel through a dug out "head race", wooden flume, or combination of the two. After turning the wheel, "spent" water was directed out of the wheel pit into a "tail race."

Workers

Serving under the direction of the ironmaster were ranks of skilled and semiskilled workers. They ranged from the company clerk and founder at the top, through intermediate levels of colliers, blacksmiths, keepers, and moulders, to the large force of woodcutters, miners, teamsters, laborers, and servants.

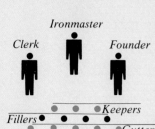

Ironmaster

Clerk   *Founder*

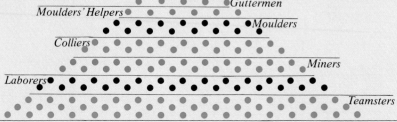

Keepers

Fillers

Guttermen

Moulders' Helpers

Moulders

Colliers

Miners

Laborers

Teamsters

Woodcutters

How Cold-Blast Charcoal Iron Was Made

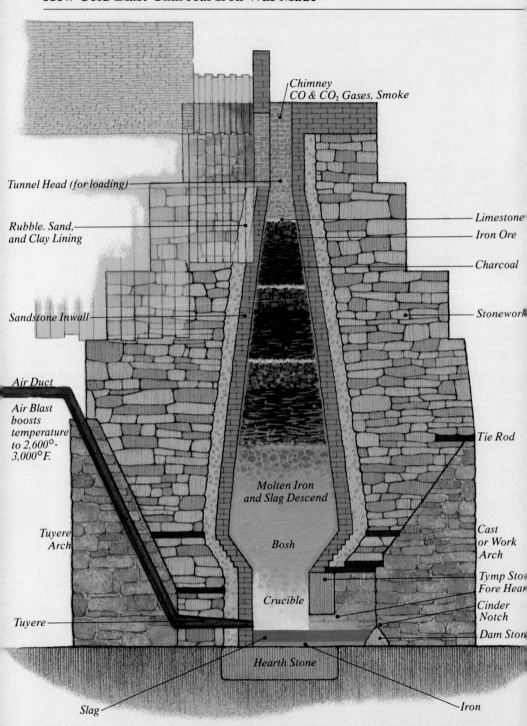

Chimney
CO & CO₂ Gases, Smoke

Tunnel Head (for loading)

Rubble. Sand, and Clay Lining

Sandstone Inwall

Air Duct

Air Blast boosts temperature to 2,600°-3,000°F.

Tuyere Arch

Tuyere

Slag

Limestone

Iron Ore

Charcoal

Stonework

Tie Rod

Molten Iron and Slag Descend

Bosh

Crucible

Cast or Work Arch

Tymp Ston Fore Hear

Cinder Notch

Dam Ston

Hearth Stone

Iron

Freeing iron from ore is a complex chemical process, in which raw materials are transformed in a controlled inferno. Minor variations in temperature and proportions make the difference between low and high quality iron. The early blast furnaces that contained this transformation shared a basic design. Thick stone outer walls and an inner lining of firebrick or sandstone withstood the extreme temperatures. From a narrow opening at the top, the inner walls sloped outward to the widest point—the "bosh"— about two-thirds down. There they sloped inward to support alternate layers of charcoal, iron ore, and limestone. At the bottom the shaft narrowed to a small chamber called the crucible. A copper "tuyere" directed air from the blast machinery into this part of the furnace. At temperatures of 2,600° to 3,000°F, the iron oxide in iron ore was "reduced" when its oxygen combined with the ascending carbon monoxide gas from the burning charcoal to produce iron and carbon dioxide. During this process, the iron absorbed carbon, which lowered its melting temperature and gave to charcoal cast iron its characteristic gray color. Limestone acted as a flux, combining with impurities in the ore to form slag. Fluid slag and iron ran down and collected on the hearth at the bottom of the furnace. The lighter slag floating on the iron was drawn off through the "cinder notch." When the clay plug in the tapping hole through the dam stone was broken, the molten iron flowed out of the furnace.

Pig Iron

Iron not cast into products was cast into rough bars convenient for transporting to market. To early observers, the pattern formed by the moulds dug in the sand floor of the cast house resembled a litter of pigs nursing at the belly of a sow. The basic product of the blast furnace became known as "pig iron," a term still used. Black, grey, and white pig iron—determined by the amount of impurities and carbon present—each had special uses. Pig iron was either cast into products at a foundry or refined into wrought iron at a refinery forge, or "finery." As the demand for iron, and then steel, grew in the 19th century, pig iron became the "foundation stone of all the iron industry."

Cast Iron

Although too brittle for tools or other implements which required ductility or toughness under sudden stress, the carbon-rich cast iron produced by a blast furnace was well suited for heavy containers and objects made to withstand fire or to radiate heat. A variety of products, including pots, pans, kettles, and stove plates, could be made at the furnace without further refining. Using skillfully carved moulds, workmen cast stove plates with intricate designs that usually featured the name of the furnace and often the date of casting, the ironmaster's name, or various mottoes and symbols. Biblical and patriotic scenes were popular during some periods.

During the Revolutionary War, some ironmasters became gunfounders, casting cannon and cannonballs for the Continental Army and Navy.

Refining Processes

Forging

At a refinery forge or "finery," pig iron bars were heated in a charcoal fire with an oxidizing air blast. Carbon and slag were removed as the finer "stirred and worked" the molten mass with an iron bar. After it was cooled and melted down twice more, the decarburized iron, called a "loupe," was repeatedly heated and pounded under a water-driven hammer to drive out more cinder and produce an internal structure of long, tough fibers—wrought iron.

Milling

Although much bar iron went directly from fineries to blacksmith shops, some was further processed for conversion into plates, rods, or nails. Early plating mills used triphammers to beat out sheets of iron. In a rolling mill, heated bar iron was passed through heavy rolls rotating in opposite directions, reducing the bar's thickness. After reheating, the iron strips were run through the "slitters," rolls fitted with sharp discs. These sheared the iron into "slit iron" rods.

Making Steel

Steel, an alloy of iron and a tiny but critical percentage of carbon, was used in products that had to withstand abnormal wear or flexing. In the cementation process, bars of wrought iron were kept at a red heat for up to 2 weeks in a "pot" packed with charcoal or charcoal dust. The bars absorbed some of the carbon (about one percent of their weight) and were converted to steel. It was called "blister steel" because of its characteristic blistered surface.

A "loupe" of pasty, red-hot iron was placed under the hammer and beaten into a "half bloom" and then re-heated and beaten into an "ancony," with a knob at each end. The ancony might be sold, but more often it was beaten out at a chafery hearth into a "merchant bar" and sold to blacksmiths and iron mills.

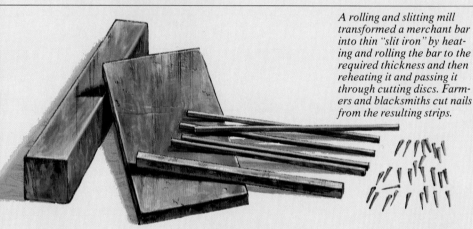

A rolling and slitting mill transformed a merchant bar into thin "slit iron" by heating and rolling the bar to the required thickness and then reheating it and passing it through cutting discs. Farmers and blacksmiths cut nails from the resulting strips.

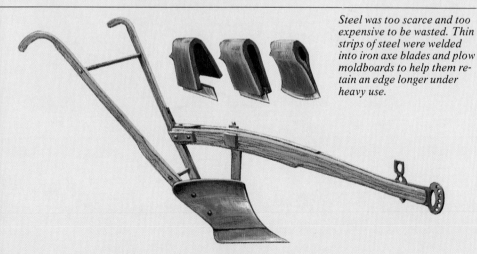

Steel was too scarce and too expensive to be wasted. Thin strips of steel were welded into iron axe blades and plow moldboards to help them retain an edge longer under heavy use.

Blacksmithing

The venerable art of black-smithing reached its zenith in the 19th century. Under the hammers of master smiths, iron yielded an amazing variety of tools, implements, and fixtures essential to the daily lives of millions of Americans. The trade especially flourished in Pennsylvania. Hundreds of forges in that state produced fine wrought iron.

Blacksmiths were valued and respected citizens known for the utility, quality, and beauty of their work. Equipped with a hand-powered bellows, hearth, anvil, hammers, tongs, punches, chisels, and forms, a blacksmith turned out horseshoes, nails, weapons, wagon tires, cooking utensils, and agricultural implements. He was also a general repair-

man who restored and re-edged tools and machinery and shod horses, mules, and oxen. Some smiths specialized in ornamental gates and grills, locks, cutlery, wagon parts, and shipbuilding items such as anchor chains. Because of the skills required and the 6-year average apprentice-ship, blacksmiths were in short supply in some regions.

Crystalline structure of wrought iron.

After refinery forge hammering.

After hammering by blacksmith.

Elongated grain allow bending.

Under the blacksmith's pounding, wrought iron's crystalline structure, already flattened and overlapped at

the refinery forge, was further lengthened. Beating drew out and aligned the fibers of slag still in the iron, making it

tougher and enhancing its usefulness for tools, farm implements, and other products subjected to heavy stress.

Pictured are the anvils and a few of the tools common to the blacksmith shop.

Anvil Chipping Block Hardy Face (round edge) Hardy Hole Pritchell Hole

Horn Heel (sharp edge) Waist Base

Swage Block

Mandrel (cone anvil)

Flatter

Flat Tongs

Ball Peen Hammer

Blacksmith's Cross Peen Sledge

18th-Century Pennsylvania Ironworks

Conditions in colonial Pennsylvania were optimal for an iron industry to take root and flourish. The colony was blessed with iron ore in abundance, large forests from which charcoal could be made, rich deposits of limestone, and numerous streams for powering water wheels. Pennsylvania's climate of religious toleration attracted entrepreneurs and skilled workmen from across the Atlantic. Starting in 1716 on Manatawny Creek in the southeastern corner of the colony, bloomery and refinery forges, blast furnaces, rolling, slitting, and plate mills, and steel furnaces spread north and west into the Susquehanna, Cumberland, and Juniata valleys. Despite largely futile attempts by Parliament to restrict colonial manufacturers, Pennsylvania was the most important iron-producing colony by the time of the Revolutionary War.

■ Iron Furnace
■ Steel Furnace
⚒ Refinery Forge or Bloomery Forge
✿ Rolling or Slitting Mill

Alliance Furnace, built in 1789-90, was the first iron furnace west of the Allegheny Mountains. The relatively small size of the tract—several hundred acres—was typical of the later ironworks built in western Pennsylvania.

Cornwall Furnace was built on Furnace Creek by Peter Grubb in 1742. The rich ore banks he worked nearby were mined for more than 200 years. Cornwall later produced shot, shells, and cannon for the Continental Army. In 1798 it was bought by Robert Coleman, whose family ran it until its final blast in 1883.

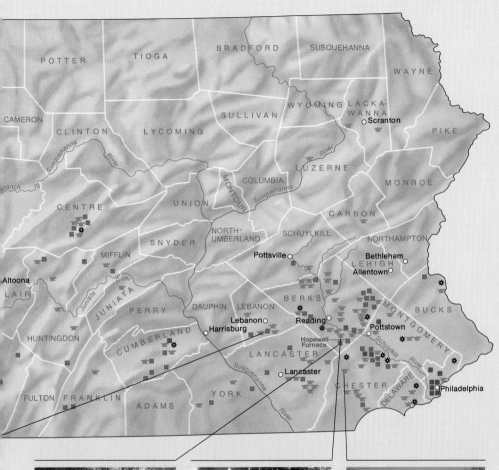

POTTER

TIOGA

BRADFORD

SUSQUEHANNA

WAYNE

CAMERON

CLINTON

LYCOMING

SULLIVAN

WYOMING LACKA-
WANNA

○ Scranton

PIKE

CENTRE

UNION

MONTOUR

COLUMBIA

LUZERNE

MONROE

MIFFLIN

SNYDER

NORTH-
UMBERLAND

SCHUYLKILL

CARBON

NORTHAMPTON

Altoona

LAIR

JUNIATA

PERRY

DAUPHIN

LEBANON

BERKS

Pottsville ○

Bethlehem
Allentown ○

LEHIGH

MONTGOMERY

BUCKS

HUNTINGDON

CUMBERLAND

Lebanon ○

Reading ○

Pottstown

Harrisburg ○

Hopewell
Furnace

Schuylkill River

LANCASTER

Lancaster ○

CHESTER

DELAWARE

Philadelphia

FULTON

FRANKLIN

ADAMS

YORK

Susquehanna River

Joanna Furnace was erected in 1792 by Samuel Potts and Thomas Rutter, grandsons of the builders of Colebrookdale, the first iron furnace in Pennsylvania. In 1847 it was converted to steam, and operated until the turn of the century.

Sands Forge was possibly one of the early forges built in the 1740s on Hay Creek in Berks County by William Bird, father of Mark Bird, builder of Hopewell Furnace.

Hibernia Ironworks began as an iron forge built in 1793 on Brandywine Creek by Samuel Downing. In 1821 the furnace and forge were bought by Charles Brooke, part-owner of Hopewell Furnace. Brooke added a rolling mill to the operation.

Part 2

Hopewell Furnace

The Story of a 19th-Century Ironmaking Community

Roots of an Industry

Of all the factors that contributed to the industrial might of 20th-century America, none was more important than the development of a flourishing iron and steel industry. The roots of this industry can be found in the hundreds of iron furnaces and forges that sprang up in the middle colonies before the Revolution and continued to operate until late in the 19th century. Hopewell Furnace in rural Berks County in eastern Pennsylvania was typical of the industry in its infancy. For more than a century, from its beginnings in 1771 to its final blast in 1883, this furnace exemplified the technological growing pains of a Nation conceived as an agricultural paradise but destined to become the industrial giant of the western world.

Hopewell is neither the oldest, the biggest, nor the last charcoal iron furnace in blast in the United States, but it is a site about which much is known and whose extensive remains are of interest to students and casual visitors alike. Founded in late colonial times, the furnace on this site supplied shot and cannon to the Continental Army and Navy during the Revolutionary War. Reflecting the economic problems of the young Republic, Hopewell led a troubled life and often changed hands until the War of 1812 gave the United States a measure of economic independence, and tariff barriers were raised to protect American industry from foreign competition. During the second quarter of the 19th century, Hopewell reached its peak of productivity, averaging each year more than 1,000 tons of pig iron and castings, mainly stoveplates and hollowware. Although this was a time of expanding markets for iron products, the leadership of Clement Brooke—by far the most able of Hopewell's ironmasters—contributed much to the furnace's success.

The idyllic scene at Hopewell today is only a pale reminder of the historical community that flourished here in the 1830s and 40s. Hopewell was then a busy industrial complex, with all the noise and dirt of 19th-century manufacturing. When the furnace was in blast, normally 24 hours a day for most of the year, the village throbbed with life: the roaring of the furnace stack, the shouts of the workmen, the water wheel monotonously clanking round and round, wagons creaking along with ore, the cast house bell periodically calling the moulders back to work. Dust, soot, and furnace odors fouled the air. The villagers accepted the noise, the dirt, the long hours, and the hard work. In many ways, workers had a better life here than did their counterparts in crowded eastern cities. There were woods, fields, and creeks nearby and the age-old rural pastimes of dances, fairs, quilting bees, corn huskings, and other community doings.

By the late 1840s, technological advances and the increasing concentration of manufacturing in urban centers were transforming the American industrial scene. Even though Hopewell remained a profitable operation for almost another 40 years, it never recovered its former prosperity. The Civil War and the subsequent industrial expansion created an enormous demand for iron and steel, and prices rose accordingly. But Hopewell and dozens of other charcoal iron furnaces were already obsolete. In 1883 the heirs of Clement Brooke finally closed Hopewell, recognizing that they could no longer compete in an industrial world based on mass production for a national market. Hopewell Furnace, and the village way of life it represented, became in a few years little more than a curiosity, a reminder that once upon a time a small part of the Nation's industrial beginnings stood here.

Overleaf: *An unbroken cycle of activities, centered on the roaring furnace stack, kept Hopewell a busy, noisy place around the clock as long as the furnace was "in blast," usually about 11 months before repairs were needed. Wagons arrived bearing fuel, limestone, and ore to feed the furnace, which was tapped twice every 24 hours. Others pulled away from the cast house with loads of cast products and pig iron for market. These tasks were performed almost continuously at Hopewell for over a century.*

Origins

The Hopewell story begins in 1770. In that year Mark Bird, an enterprising and ambitious Pennsylvanian, finished buying several large tracts of land in Berks and Chester Counties on which to establish an iron-making community. About 30 years old and the son of a successful ironmaster, he was hoping to follow in the steps of other Pennsylvania entrepreneurs who for half a century had been exploiting the colony's abundant natural resources—ore, forests, and water—to build a prosperous iron industry.

The roots of this industry go back nearly to the founding of this country. In 1621, upriver from Jamestown, Virginia, transplanted Englishmen made the first attempt on these shores to produce iron. Twenty-five years later a more successful ironworks was established at Saugus, Massachusetts. Soon ironworks began to dot the New England landscape, spreading southward along rivers and creeks near surface deposits of iron ore. The earliest ironworks were bloomery forges, in which forgemen produced a crude wrought iron by heating ore with a bellows over a charcoal fire and hammering the mass (called a bloom) into shape.

Bloomeries were gradually replaced by blast furnaces, which produced iron from which most of the impurities were smelted out. These furnaces, common in England and Europe at the time, were a new order of technology in colonial America. They were more highly organized and operated on a far larger scale than the bloomeries they supplanted. Their processes centered on a large, pyramidal stone furnace, usually 30 or more feet high, in which ore, charcoal, and limestone were cooked together for hours, yielding a high-quality molten iron.

These "iron plantations," as they were often called, were more than just forerunners of the factories and mills of a generation later. They were in fact entire villages that had sprung up in proximity to the resources on which they depended: iron ore near the surface, a dependable water supply to power the air blast, extensive hardwood forests for charcoal, and limestone for flux.

Pennsylvania had these resources in abundance, and by the mid-18th century it had become the leading iron-producing colony in British America. In 1771 well over 50 furnaces and forges were operating in that colony alone, and American pig iron commanded a high price in Britain. Mark Bird's father was typical of this first generation of Pennsylvania ironmasters. After learning his trade by working at a number of forges, he went into business for himself and built Hopewell Forge near the Schuylkill River at what is now Birdsboro. At the time of his death in 1761, he owned two forges and a furnace and more than 3,000 acres.

Young Mark Bird took over the family business after his father's death and soon began to expand it. Energetic like his father, he bought into a new furnace in Lancaster County and picked up more land in Berks and Chester Counties. By 1763 he owned more than 8,000 acres. Continuing to accumulate property, he eventually added two important tracts, the Hopewell and Jones Good Luck mines, to his holdings. By 1770 he was one of the largest landowners in Berks County, owning thousands of acres of woodland, iron mines, and water rights. For a new furnace he chose a site near French Creek in the southern part of the county, 5 miles from his father's forge near the Schuylkill and only a few miles from Hopewell mine.

According to the date on a cornerstone, Hopewell Furnace was built in 1771. The following year it was in full operation, as attested by a stove plate bearing the imprint "Mark Bird—Hopewell Furnace—1772." The name Hopewell was presumably taken from his father's Hopewell Forge. This was a popular name for ironworks in colonial America and often used in Virginia and New Jersey. The activities at Bird's furnace during its first 13 years of operation are largely a mystery today since only records back to 1784 have survived. Its operation was unquestionably similar to other Pennsylvania furnaces of its day. The requisite raw materials—ore, forests, limestone, and water—were all close by. Moreover, there was both skilled and unskilled labor in the vicinity because of the recent multiplication of ironworks in eastern Pennsylvania and a network of roads, even if primitive, over which iron could move to nearby forges and stoveplates to market in Philadelphia and other cities.

Bird constructed his furnace against a hill a little north of French Creek. Two water courses (called head races) furnished water for power. The east race ran about a mile from Baptism Creek, and the west race ran 2 miles from mountain springs. According to local tradition, the races were constructed by slave labor. This is likely since Mark Bird, who owned about 18 blacks, was the largest slaveowner in Berks County at that time. The races brought water to an overshot wheel beside the furnace. During Bird's tenure at Hopewell this wheel probably operated a pair of large leather bellows, since blowing tubs were not used in American ironmaking until later in the 18th century. The bellows forced a cold blast of air into an opening (called the "tuyere") at the base of the furnace, causing the fire to burn at smelting temperature ($2,600°$ to $3,000°$ F.). The molten iron was tapped from the front of the furnace and either run into sand beds as "pigs" or into moulds for stoveplates, pots, sash weights, tools, or (during the Revolutionary War) cannon and shot. A tail race carried the spent water from the wheel into French Creek.

Because of his business and political

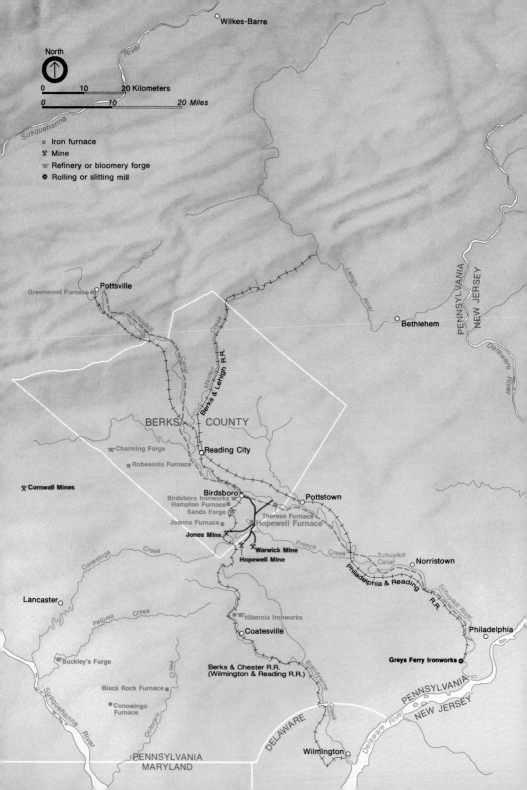

North

0   10   20 Kilometers

0   10   20 Miles

■ Iron furnace
✕ Mine
⚓ Refinery or bloomery forge
✿ Rolling or slitting mill

Wilkes-Barre

Susquehanna   River

Susquehanna

Pottsville

Greenwood Furnace

Schuylkill   Canal

Maiden   Creek

Berks & Lehigh R.R.

Lehigh   River

Bethlehem

PENNSYLVANIA

NEW JERSEY

Delaware   River

BERKS   COUNTY

Charming Forge

Reading City

Robesonia Furnace

✕ Cornwall Mines

Birdsboro
Birdsboro Ironworks
Hampton Furnace
Sands Forge
Joanna Furnace

Theresa Furnace
Hopewell Furnace

Pottstown

Jones Mine

Warwick Mine

Hopewell Mine

French   Creek

Schuylkill   Canal

Norristown

Philadelphia & Reading   R.R.

Schuylkill   River

Conestoga   Creek

Lancaster

Pequea   Creek

Hibernia Ironworks

Coatesville

Philadelphia

Greys Ferry Ironworks ✿

Buckley's Forge

Black Rock Furnace

Conowingo Furnace

Octorara   Creek

Berks & Chester R.R.
(Wilmington & Reading R.R.)

Brandywine   Creek

Susquehanna   River

DELAWARE

Delaware   River

PENNSYLVANIA

NEW JERSEY

PENNSYLVANIA
MARYLAND

Wilmington

interests in Birdsboro, Reading, and Philadelphia, Bird probably spent little time at Hopewell, leaving operations in the hands of a resident manager. He probably constructed other buildings during this time, though we cannot be sure exactly what.

Like his fellow ironmasters, Bird strongly resented the British Iron Act of 1750, which limited the American iron industry to the production of pig and bar iron that could be, according to prevailing mercantile doctrine, reworked by British forges into finished products and exported to the colonies. Although the act was easily evaded, the restriction led many ironmasters to oppose all imperial regulations. After Massachusetts and Virginia, Pennsylvania was probably the most radical of the colonies in resisting such British enactments as the Stamp Act and the Tea Act.

Even before hostilities broke out at Lexington and Concord in April 1775, Mark Bird was a member of the Pennsylvania Committee of Correspondence and the Pennsylvania Provincial Conference. Both were radical groups and increasingly active in the movement for independence. After the Declaration of Independence, he served first as lieutenant-colonel and then as colonel of the Second Battalion of Berks County militia. He was also elected to the State Assembly that enacted the liberal constitution of 1776 and was a judge of the Berks County court. He was now clearly one of the leading patriots of eastern Pennsylvania and an example of the prominent and wealthy Americans at the front of the revolutionary movement. As a militia colonel, he not only was obliged to train his men but also to outfit them at his own expense with uniforms, tents, and provisions. After George Washington's defeat at the battle of Brandywine in September 1777, Bird marched his men to the relief of the Continental Army, prepared to oppose a

British advance up the Schuylkill Valley, which would threaten not only his own but other ironworks.

During the ensuing 6 years, the war drew no closer to Berks County. Bird's principal contribution to the cause was not as a military leader but as a supplier of munitions and matériel to the beleaguered American forces. As Deputy Quartermaster General of Pennsylvania, he was responsible for providing food and equipment for American forces. During the hard winter of 1778 he shipped a thousand barrels of flour down the Schuylkill to Washington's troops at Valley Forge. His ironworks, including Hopewell Furnace, supplied cannon and shot throughout the war to the Continental Army and armed several Continental frigates.

Congress recognized the contributions of Bird's ironworkers to the war. In June 1777 the Board of War discharged 11 of his workmen from the militia, saying that "they are of more extensive uses to the continent in their employment as artificers . . . [for] the works must stand still if these workmen march out with the Militia." Yet like most creditors of the new United States government, Bird had difficulty getting paid by the virtually bankrupt Congress. The payments he received were infrequent and insufficient. Congress advanced him $2,000 in 1776 to cast cannon, and twice issued him powder "to prove the cannon he has made." In 1780, at one of the lowest points in the revolutionary struggle, Congress authorized payment to him of $125,000 for "military stores" and other work, but there is no record that payment was actually made. No one can say how much shot and cannon were made at Hopewell, but since this was Bird's only furnace at the time, it undoubtedly was the source of his ordnance.

After the war, Bird asked Congress to give him the great chain strung across the Hudson River at West Point to obstruct British warships. This, he said, would be an acceptable partial payment. Congress denied his request, maintaining that he was only one of many creditors. Nor was this Bird's only financial problem. Along with many of his fellow ironmasters, he had over-expanded his business during and after the war and was hard hit when the national economy faltered. Besides his interests in Hopewell Furnace and Birdsboro Forge, which included a slitting mill and a steel furnace, he was a partner in a number of other ironworks in Pennsylvania and with his brother-in-law James Wilson (a distinguished lawyer and signer of the Constitution) owned an ironworks near Trenton, New Jersey, at the falls of the Delaware. He was an investor in the schooner *United States,* which was outfitted for the China trade, but its maiden voyage was unsuccessful. He apparently closed down his Berks County ironworks after the war, for in 1784 he appealed to the county for a reduction in taxes.

Mark Bird never recovered from the economic downturn of the 1780s. Floods and fire damaged his works at Hopewell and Birdsboro, and he suffered a reverse at the Trenton ironworks. After Dutch bankers refused to lend him money, he was forced to mortgage the Hopewell property. In an act of desperation in 1786, the depth of the depression, he put the Hopewell and Birdsboro properties up for sale—4,000 acres, 5,000 cords of wood, and 800 loads of iron ore—but was unable to find a buyer.

Two years later "Hopewell plantation" was auctioned off to James Old and Cadwallader Morris, and Mark Bird fled from his remaining creditors to North Carolina, a well-known debtor's refuge. When that State's legislature denied his petition for bankruptcy, Bird turned to farming for a living. Meanwhile, the Hopewell property passed through several hands, but the furnace was not profitable, even though in 1789 it was the second largest of 14 Pennsylvania furnaces in operation, with a capacity of 700 tons annually. James Wilson bought the furnace in 1794 to supply his numerous forges with pig iron, but two years later the property again went on the block, and Wilson, like Bird, fled to North Carolina. In 1800 the partnership of Daniel Buckley and his brothers-in-law Matthew and Thomas Brooke bought the furnace and for the next 83 years the two families owned and operated it.

Mark Bird was now languishing, virtually forgotten, in North Carolina. After some of his debts were paid off in 1796, he returned to Berks County for a short visit, but soon went back into exile. In 1807, when he was 68 and in failing health, he wrote two plaintive letters, one to the Philadelphia physician Benjamin Rush, a former friend, and the other to Matthew Brooke, one of the new owners. His letter to Brooke declared: "I shall not think well of the Iron masters, when they come to know my Situation, if they do not fall on some mode . . . to relieve me, either by lone, or other wise, they know I was Ruined, by the Warr, it was not Drunkeness, Idleness or want of Industry." His letter to Rush was in the same tone: "I was Bankrupt by the Vile unnatural war, and never has been Able to get anything of Acct. in my hands since. . . . There is no doubt my principle ruin, was by the Warr and Depretiation." His request for aid from his former friends was rejected by Rush, who noted on the back: "declined soliciting relief for him as all his friends of 1776 were dead or reduced." Mark Bird died in North Carolina in 1816, but the furnace he founded at Hopewell continued to live on for many decades, a monument to the energy and vision of its creator.

Daniel Buckley became a Hopewell partner in 1800, beginning a family connection with the furnace and the Brooke family that lasted almost a century. With Matthew and Thomas Brooke, he successfully guided Hopewell through lawsuits and heavy debt, which kept the furnace out of blast from 1808 to 1816. Buckley died in 1828, to be succeeded as partner by his son Matthew Brooke Buckley and then by his grandson Edward S. Buckley.

Years of Prosperity

The year 1800 was a landmark for Hopewell Furnace and the Nation. In Buckley and the Brookes, Hopewell had owners who took an active part in the business. On the national scene, Thomas Jefferson's election as president, and its acceptance by his political opponents, was a signal that the Republic could survive and prosper in spite of partisan and sectional wrangling. Both Hopewell and the Nation stood on the threshold of an era of prosperity and economic growth.

The Jefferson administration was not sympathetic to industrial development. It preferred an agrarian economy underpinned by foreign trade. Nevertheless, during the ensuing decades manufacturing continued to grow in the United States, particularly in the Northeast. The renewal of worldwide warfare between England and France in 1803 seriously interfered with American trade, especially the importation of manufactured goods from Europe. In retaliation, President Jefferson imposed an embargo on all foreign trade in 1807 because he could get no concessions from the warring powers. Finally in 1812 the United States went to war with England, mainly over maritime grievances. The unavailability of foreign goods left a gap that American industry now began to fill. New England's textile mills were the principal beneficiaries of the embargo, but ironworks were also encouraged. After peace finally came in 1815, Congress enacted protective tariffs to foster these "infant industries" and help make the United States economically more self-sufficient. Over the next quarter-century, despite two serious business panics (as recessions were called in those days), the American iron industry continued to flourish, as the success of Hopewell Furnace illustrates.

When Buckley and the Brookes purchased Hopewell Furnace in 1800, their future hardly appeared bright. The purchase price was £10,000.* This gave them title to more than 5,000 acres, two mines, and the furnace, including "all houses–out-houses–buildings–improvements–quarries–woods–waters–watercourses–rights, liberties, etc." The purchase price was paid almost entirely in transferable bonds for future redemption, making interest on this debt a continuing obligation of the partners. Other debts were also incurred as the furnace began operation, and it appeared at times as if the partners could not pay their creditors, let alone make a profit. The cost of capital improvements was another drag on profits, for the furnace required renovation. That they eventually succeeded was due in part to their previous experience in the iron industry. Matthew Brooke had helped manage Hopewell Furnace for a short time before the purchase, his brother Thomas had been involved in ironworks in Montgomery County, while Daniel Buckley was a successful owner of furnaces and forges in Lancaster County. The partners, whether resident at Hopewell, Birdsboro, Buckley Forge, or Philadelphia, corresponded regularly and generally agreed on business tactics.

The furnace records after 1800 contain extensive evidence of major repairs. The two bellows were repaired in 1801, and 3 years later the furnace was renovated. A new charcoal house was also built on the furnace bank next to the stack. Probably the most important work was the remodeling of the water wheel and head race system. The original east head race remained in use, but because of a controversy over water rights—a claimant had diverted the water flowing through his land—the west head race had to be abandoned.

In its place a new and shorter west head race was constructed from a dam on French Creek. This brought the water to the wheel at a lower elevation, and so the original north-south overshot wheel was changed to an east-west breast wheel, the type operating today. In 1807 a series of disasters struck the new dam. An April flood breached it. Three months after repairs, it was broken again. Finally in September it was destroyed by lightning. Meantime, the partners were constantly losing money from their operations, for the value of iron produced barely met the costs of wages and salaries. In 1808, as a national recession stemming from the trade embargo compounded their personal problems, the Buckley-Brooke partnership closed down Hopewell Furnace and did not put it back in blast until 1816, when the war was over.

Litigation over land titles, a heritage from the early history of Hopewell Furnace, was probably the most important reason why the partners shut down operations.* When Mark Bird first acquired the property, he was aware that his title was cloudy but chose to ignore it. Peter Meyer, one of Bird's former employees, testified in 1810 that when he approached the ironmaster to buy 40 acres for his own use, Bird replied: "I can't give you a good right for it & I suppose you would not wish to buy it unless I could give you a

*The roots of the Hopewell litigation went back to the original 1742 grant by John and Richard Penn, sons of William Penn, the original proprietor of the colony. Mark Bird acquired land within this grant, as did Matthias Kahler, who in 1801 filed suit against Buckley and the Brookes to eject them from more than 300 acres of woodland. A few years later the Penn heirs sued both Kahler and the Hopewell partners, claiming 1,000 acres with the "appurtenances situate in Union Township." The owners of nearby Warwick Furnace were involved in the latter suit, obviously hoping to acquire woodland which would give them a competitive advantage over the Hopewell partners.

*At this time most American business transactions still used the British expression of "pounds." The pounds in question were Pennsylvania pounds, worth only a little more than half a British pound.

good right. You live on the land now & as long as I & you can agree, you may still live on there."

While the court was deciding who owned the original Bird land, no wood could be cut or charcoal made on it, and Hopewell Furnace had to curtail operations until the suit was resolved. Daniel Buckley, in a letter to Matthew Brooke, was dejected by the prospect: "I am endeavoring to reconcile myself to the most Disastrous Consequences . . . my Business ever since I have been concerned in Berks County has been going Backwards and unless something meraculous turns up I fear I shall be ruined. . . . My mind has almost sunk under my Trouble." The litigation was costly, since appeals were carried by both parties to higher courts. The lawyer for the Buckley-Brooke partnership noted that "the defendants . . . was prevented from the use of the furnace for want of sufficient wood, and were obliged to expend large sums of money to defend and carry on the tryals. . . . During which time the works etc. went into decay and after the Decision . . . Cost near $8000 to repair before the furnace could be of any use." Most of these lawsuits were settled by 1815. The Hopewell partners had to surrender 239 acres to one claimant, but won the other lawsuits. The owners of Hopewell Furnace, with a clear title to their land, were finally able to resume operations.

When the furnace was put back in blast in 1816, the United States was embarking upon a new era of economic expansion. Peace reigned in Europe again, and international trade began to flourish, stimulating the growing American economy. But European manufactured goods, dumped on the American market, threatened the domestic industry that had grown up during the decade of war and embargo. Besides the protective tariffs enacted by Congress to nurture the new industries,

both the Federal government and the States took other steps to encourage economic development: Congress created a national bank with branches throughout the Nation to provide a more uniform currency and credit system, and it encouraged the construction of turnpikes and canals to help create a national market. This "transportation revolution" contributed to the spread of new industrial techniques and the consequent division of labor. Renewed immigration from Europe, bringing a fresh supply of labor, skilled and unskilled, also provided a vital ingredient for the industrial revolution in the United States. American industrial development still lagged behind that of Western Europe, but within a half-century it would challenge the Old World and in less than a century would surpass it.

Hopewell Furnace was an example of this process of modernization. The Buckley-Brooke partners not only put the furnace back into operation, but they also introduced technical advances that improved its efficiency and productivity. As early as 1805 they installed a stamping mill to crush the discarded slag around the furnace in order to recover the small deposits of iron imbedded in it. Because this iron found a ready market at nearby forges, Daniel Buckley urged Matthew Brooke to repair the mill when it broke down, arguing that "when it can be got with so little trouble why is it neglected?" During the long shutdown of the furnace, the stamping mill provided virtually the only income for Hopewell. It ceased operation in 1817, probably because new methods had reduced the amount of iron in the slag.

Undoubtedly the most significant improvement was the addition of new blast machinery. Wooden blowing tubs with internal pistons replaced the outmoded and relatively inefficient leather bellows. Powered by the water wheel, these blowing tubs forced air through a system of valves into the opening at the base of the furnace. The efficiency of the pistons was raised by the installation of "patent elastic piston springs" invented by a local millwright, and a wheelhouse was constructed to protect the machinery from the weather. These and other improvements, as well as the rising demand for iron, increased the productivity of the furnace during the next two decades, raising profits in spite of a 3-year depression that followed the business panic of 1819. For example, over 30 percent more iron was produced in 1820 than 15 years earlier, while the monetary value of the product increased nearly 50 percent. Five years later annual production nearly doubled, with a proportional increase in income. By the mid-1830s, the most productive and profitable period of Hopewell's history, the income of the furnace had doubled again, despite only a 20-percent increase in productivity. Even allowing for higher costs and inflation, Hopewell Furnace was obviously a remarkably profitable enterprise.

Technological improvements are not the only explanation for this success. The decision of the partners to concentrate on industrial castings rather than pig iron was even more important. Hopewell had always manufactured stoveplates and small utensils, but this now became its principal activity. In 1817 a cupola—a small smelter made of sheet iron—was constructed near the furnace to resmelt pig iron from the furnace into small castings such as sash weights, pots, and mold boards. The major productive activity at Hopewell now became the manufacture of stoveplates, which were shipped to an expanding market ranging from New Hampshire to Maryland. The improvement of turnpikes east to Philadelphia and west to Lancaster and Harrisburg, then the construction of the Schuylkill and Union Canals, and finally the completion of the Reading Railroad all helped connect Hopewell to markets. With a resident agent in Philadelphia and a growing reputation for quality production, Hopewell was soon faced with the welcome problem of demand outstripping its ability to supply this popular item.

Cast-iron stoves had been growing in popularity since early in the 18th century when German immigrants began to arrive in numbers, many of them with treasured patterns for stoveplates based on Biblical motifs. Ironmasters gladly cast stoveplates to order from these carved patterns, and soon found a new market among the English, whose habit of heating and cooking with open fireplaces was wasteful of expensive firewood. The advantages of the freestanding stove were soon widely evident. Benjamin Franklin's famous invention of the "Pennsylvania furnace," which made fireplaces far more efficient, further increased the demand for cast-iron stoves.

Stove technology advanced rapidly in the early 1800s. Ironmasters developed the 10-plate stove, which was a considerable improvement over the primitive 6-plate, box-like stove that Mark Bird and others had manufactured. These new stoves had grates and could burn anthracite (hard) coal as well as wood. The second major improvement was in the method of casting. Flask-casting replaced the 18th-century method of open-sand casting. In open-sand casting, a wooden pattern was pressed into the sand in front of the furnace. Molten iron was run into this bed to cool, and then the plate was trimmed and brushed clean. Flask-casting used a box filled with damp sand to form a mould around a pattern. When the iron hardened, the box was opened and the plate was removed and cleaned. The finished stoveplates were then crated and shipped to retailers, who bolted them together. From 1825 to 1844 stoveplates were Hopewell's most lucrative product.

The Products of Hopewell

The Hopewell Stove

The casting of iron stove plates was a mainstay of Hopewell's operation until 1844. These plates were shipped to dealers, who furnished the rods, bolts, and sheet iron to assemble stoves. Berks County was a center of stove casting, and Hopewell was well-known for its high-quality coal and wood-fueled stoves, sold as far north as Portsmouth, New Hampshire, and south to Baltimore. Many were cast with "Hopewell Furnace" prominent on the side plates, while others featured the name of the dealer. From intricate wooden patterns—carved at Hopewell or furnished by the customer— moulders cast stove plates with elaborate floral, animal, and classical motifs. Some patterns were traditional Old World designs brought over by immigrants. Others reflected current events: The New Orleans Victory Stove, Perry's Victory Stove, Don't Give Up the Ship Stove, and Peace Stove were some of the relatively short-lived styles to come out of the War

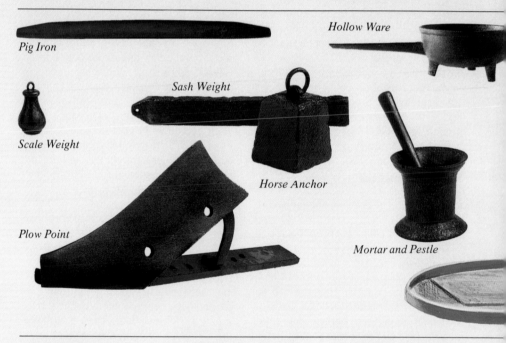

Pig Iron

Hollow Ware

Scale Weight

Sash Weight

Horse Anchor

Plow Point

Mortar and Pestle

Castings and Pigs

Although Hopewell's name was often associated with stove plates, a vast array of items issued from the cast house. Most profitable were the finished cast products: pots, skillets, kettles, flat irons, wheels, mill screws, apple mill nuts, clock weights, anvils, hammers, grates, moldboards, and grindstone wheels. Farm machinery inventions in the 1820s called for new types of castings, such as those for threshing and shelling machines. Hopewell even produced door frames and "peepholes" for the new State penitentiary in 1826-27. During the Revolutionary War, Hopewell furnished the Continental Army with 4-, 9-, and 12-pounder cannon, plus cannon shot.

Throughout its history, Hopewell also produced pig iron bars. Pig iron was generally of a slightly different composition than the finished cast products, depending on the quality of and impurities in the ore used, and the manner of smelting. Pigs varied in size, but one found at Hopewell is 4 feet long and 5½ by 2 inches at one end. "Gate metal," left over from the flask-casting process, and imperfect castings were sold with the pig iron to forges, where they were refined and turned into wrought iron products.

of 1812. As the war fervor died down, these were replaced with Flower Pot, Hornet and Peacock, Shepherd, and Fox Chase styles. From the simple 6-plate stove cast in the early years, Hopewell progressed to more than a hundred different sizes and types, including oval, cannon, square, and Franklin stoves. In the late 18th century, the development of closed flask casting, allowing lighter, curved plates, led to the 10-plate circular stove. This type became Hopewell's most popular stove. The high point was in 1839, when 5,152 stoves of all types were produced.

Based on principles used in earlier European stoves, Franklin's original freestanding fireplace called for a system of baffles to extract the maximum amount of heat. The name "Franklin Stove" was later attached to inserts which increased the efficiency of masonry fireplaces. Hopewell produced at least four styles of Franklin Stoves.

The circular stove (here, the 10-plate cooking model) was cast in nine sizes and with a number of different patterns. Variations included a sunken bottom and a boiler top to accommodate a kettle. It featured a lower fire box and upper oven that could bake meat, bread, cakes, and pies.

39

Moving Iron to Markets

Transportation costs could determine success or failure for an iron furnace. For the first 54 years of Hopewell's operation, wagons drawn by oxen or horses over dirt roads were the primary means of transportation to market, although some iron was transported by boat on the Schuylkill River. Hopewell was built near an existing road from Reading to Coventry Forge. Mark Bird provided his own connecting road and built another private road to the Hopewell Mine in 1772. Other important roads were built or realigned to connect Hopewell with the Jones Mine (1804), the Schuylkill River (1809), Birdsboro (1815), Warwick Mine (1825), and the Schuylkill Canal (1827). Hopewell's transport costs were inflated by turnpike and bridge tolls on these roads. Furnace workers often had to repair public roads with slag, although the company could deduct the cost from its road taxes. After the development of other means of transport, Hopewell still needed roads to get the product to loading points.

The opening of the Schuylkill Canal in 1825 gave Hopewell a cheaper, generally faster means of transport. By 1836, most of the furnace's products moved this way to market, although when the canal froze, ship-pers were forced to transport products to Philadelphia by wagon. The canal altered Hopewell's pattern of distribution. Most of the cast items went to Philadelphia, Wilmington, New York, Boston, and Portsmouth, and pig iron was sold to local forges. The traditional markets to the west received little attention.

Rail service was available to Hopewell with the opening of the Reading to Philadelphia Railroad along the Schuylkill River. Hopewell's first shipments to Philadelphia by rail were in 1839. By 1842 all of its stoves were shipped this way. Rail transport cost slightly more, but it was much faster.

Hopewell, like other furnaces, both designed its own stove patterns and reproduced patterns brought to the furnace. After the War of 1812, patriotic designs depicting Perry's victory at Lake Erie, Jackson's triumph at New Orleans, and other themes from a generally inglorious war were popular with customers, but floral and Biblical designs were still in demand. In the early 1830s nearly a hundred different patterns were produced at Hopewell.

Hopewell's success during the 1830s and '40s can be credited to Clement Brooke, resident manager and ironmaster from 1816 until his retirement in 1848. He found new markets for the furnace's products and was responsible for the decision to concentrate on castings rather than pig iron. His formal education was rudimentary, but his practical education embraced all aspects of furnace operations. Born in 1784, he went to work as assistant clerk at 16, when his father and uncles took over Hopewell Furnace. A few years later he worked part-time at the furnace at night, supervising the filling of the stack for a blast. In 1804, at the age of 20, he was made clerk of the furnace, and in that position of responsibility kept records of all operations. While the furnace was shut down from 1808 to 1816, he was caretaker of the property, charged with operating the stamping mill and supervising general maintenance. When the furnace resumed operations in 1816, Clement Brooke was appointed resident manager at a salary of $600 a year plus free residence in the ironmaster's mansion. His wife was given an annual housekeeping allowance of $70 to maintain the establishment. Food and other normal household expenses were provided by the company, as well as expenses incurred in pursuing furnace business away from Hopewell. After the death of his father in 1831, Clement inherited a one-sixth share of the furnace,

and in 1833 purchased, with his brother Charles, a share of the Buckley interest.

During his tenure as ironmaster, Clement Brooke made many improvements in the property. He added a rear wing with cellar and kitchen to the ironmaster's house in 1825, and 4 years later a southwest wing. He needed the space for his official "family" (including servants), which had increased from 6 to 15 in less than 20 years. An enlarged spring house, bake ovens, and a formal garden also appeared near the Big House during these years, and as more workers were hired, tenant houses were built within walking distance of the furnace complex. Since Mark Bird's day, the village had had a blacksmith shop and a barn for livestock and wagons, but the office and company store next to Brooke's dwelling was now enlarged to meet the needs of the growing community. During his tenure a schoolhouse was built across the creek from the furnace, and about 1837 a wheelwright set up shop in the village. Under Brooke the labor force increased by half. As ironmaster at Hopewell furnace for three decades, Clement Brooke was liked and respected by his employees, his partners, and his customers, earning a reputation as one of the best ironmasters in Pennsylvania.

Clement Brooke's success was echoed by the experience of other early 19th-century American entrepreneurs. When the Nation celebrated its 50th birthday in 1826, the prevailing tone in oratory and in the press was one of unquestioning optimism about the future. Previous sectional and political animosities were transcended by a sense of national purpose and a belief in an American mission to enlighten the world. Universal white male suffrage and the election of Andrew Jackson in 1828 appeared to herald a new era of democratic nationalism, but this "age of the common man" was deceptive. As "laissez-faire" became the dominant eco-

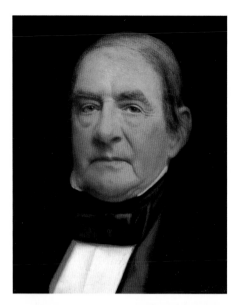

Clement Brooke, Hopewell's Manager, 1816-48, and partner, 1827-61.

Maria Church Brooke, wife of Clement Brooke.

nomic principle, the government drastically reduced its role as regulator and protector of American business. The chief beneficiaries were those who had capital or access to it. The corporate form of business organization was beginning to supplant proprietorships and partnerships, contributing to the growth of monopoly and the consequent lessening of business competition. Even though this development did not reach its peak until after the Civil War, its effects were increasingly apparent in the United States by mid-century.

These changes did not yet affect Hopewell Furnace. The iron industry was extremely competitive, and quality of product was as important as improved marketing techniques in guaranteeing profits. To maintain a high level of production, Brooke bought more woodland and sought other sources of iron ore, while continuing to rely upon the rich veins at the Hopewell and Jones mines. As early as 1821 he was buying ore from the Warwick mines in Chester County, paying a royalty based on the tonnage of iron produced. Eight years later Hopewell became part owner of these mines. In the 1840s Brooke was a partner in the Warwick Furnace Reserve in Berks and Chester Counties, and had the right to search for ore anywhere in the 20,000-acre tract. Meantime, the ironmaster was managing to increase production without any sacrifice of quality.

The decade of the 1830s was the most prosperous in the history of Hopewell. An 1832 Treasury Department report to Congress described the furnace: "Men employed—168, Supposed No. of dependents —800, No. of horses—84, Pig Metal—1,000 Tons, Castings—700 Tons." Over the next 5 years the proportion of castings to pig iron increased until four times as much of the former was being made as the latter. Not only did the volume of stoveplate casting increase, but the growing mechanization of agriculture led to a demand for plow castings, mold boards, threshing machines, shelling machines, and windmill irons. The furnace also continued to produce sash weights, wagon iron, anvils, griddles, and grates.

The average length of time the furnace was in blast during the 1830s was 11½ months. It was shut down only when the supply of charcoal was exhausted or the furnace inwalls needed repair. During the celebrated "long blast" of 1836-37, the furnace operated continuously for 445 days—from January 3, 1836 to April 10, 1837—producing 1,169 tons of mixed castings and several hundred tons of pig iron. Because this was a period of spiraling inflation, iron prices were high, as Brooke wrote a customer: "the supposed Price of stove Casting will be from $100 to $110 per ton. . . . We presume castings will be very scarce in the market next season, Pig Iron is now selling on the Furnace Banks from $50 to $60 per ton and a Supply cannot be got at any Price, we intend making a winter Blast and must know who we are to supply."

In early 1837 widespread bank failures, the bankruptcy of international traders, and a general stagnation of business brought the boom to a sudden halt. The Panic of 1837 was the most severe depression in American history up to that time. It lasted for more than 5 years and created massive unemployment and economic distress, particularly in the eastern cities. Although Hopewell Furnace survived, its market shrank in comparison with the mid-30s. In 1844, probably because of declining demand and increased costs, Clement Brooke ended large-scale stoveplate casting. During its last four decades Hopewell mainly produced pig iron, for which there was a growing demand in a rapidly industrializing society. The furnace managed to turn a profit through most of those years, but it never again enjoyed the prosperity of the 1825-44 period, the peak of its success.

In 1848, at the age of 64, Clement Brooke retired as ironmaster at Hopewell Furnace and moved into a new house in neighboring Pottstown. He was a wealthy man for this time: besides his half share in Hopewell, he owned shares in five other iron furnaces and forges. He also had an interest in coal mines in Schuylkill County and owned stock in several railroad companies. In 1859 he moved to Philadelphia, where he died 2 years later at the age of 76. Clement Brooke's association with Hopewell spanned more than a half-century, a period marked by far-reaching changes in the structure of society and the economy of the expanding nation. His career epitomized the growing pains as well as the successes of industrial capitalism during the infancy of the American industrial revolution.

Life and Work at Hopewell Furnace

During his term as ironmaster at Hopewell Furnace, Clement Brooke sat at the top of the community's social pyramid, sharing profits, power, and policy only with his absentee partners. Unlike most of his predecessors and successors, he was an integral part of the community and lived in the Big House with his family and other dependents. He took an interest in all aspects of the business and was readily accessible to his employees and customers. If the furnace was idle, the Brookes occasionally escaped to Philadelphia in winter, but otherwise Hopewell was their home. As ironmaster he was not only the principal executive officer of the business, but chief engineer, personnel officer, and sales manager as well.

The ironmaster's mansion was at once the family home, the business headquarters, a boarding house, and a social center. The house was well designed for these functions, especially after Brooke added two wings to the original structure. The main floor had four large rooms, including a kitchen and a broad stairway that led to six bedrooms on the second floor. The ground floor, accessible from a rear courtyard, contained a dining room, kitchen, and storage rooms, while a four-room attic provided quarters for the servants. Of the seven fireplaces, two were primarily for cooking, the others for heating. The 1830 census listed nine males and six females in the household, four of the latter being "Negro servants." Among other occupants were the company clerk, who frequently lodged and boarded there, any apprentices bound to him, and, when the furnace was in blast, single workers, who took their meals in the basement dining room. The mansion was also regularly visited by relatives, customers, or business acquaintances (since the only public accommodations were miles away) who had to be entertained properly. Serving so many functions, the house was usually crowded and seldom a quiet family retreat.

The ironmaster's wife oversaw all the housekeeping functions, including domestic activities in other buildings near the mansion. Bread and pastries were regularly baked in outdoor ovens behind the basement kitchen, while meat was preserved in a nearby smokehouse. A spring house, first built in 1806 and later enlarged, not only provided water for the Big House, but was used for laundering, soap making, butchering, and cooling milk and butter. On the terraced hillside north of the mansion were extensive gardens, grape arbors, orchards, and an icehouse and greenhouse. A privy with separate stalls for family and servants was nearby.

While Clement Brooke looked after the furnace, his wife supervised the servants. During this period there was comparatively little turnover among household employees, most of whom were members of furnace workers' families, and things generally ran smoothly during her tenure. Wages for domestic service ranged from 50¢ to $1.50 a week, with full board and room provided. Some housemaids had accounts at the furnace store, and often went into debt buying shoes, shawls, hats, and fabrics. Domestic service at Hopewell was not necessarily a dead end, as it often was in eastern cities, because of the plentiful supply of single men at the furnace. Many a servant girl married a worker and settled down as a respected matron in the community.

Second in importance to the ironmaster was the company clerk, who not only kept the books for the furnace but managed it in the ironmaster's absence. No educational qualifications were required for this job. Clerks were chosen for their intelligence and common sense, skill with figures, and ability to write a legible hand. Most, like John Benson, a former miner, were handpicked by the ironmaster, but John Church got the job partly because he was Mrs. Brooke's nephew. Whether a clerk earned the job or not, he kept it out of merit, for he performed a vital task for the ironmaster. The company clerk recorded all the furnace's financial transactions: the costs of labor, materials, and transportation, taxes and license fees, income from sales, payments to partners, and the expenses of repairs and capital improvements. But the furnace records do not answer all the questions we are interested in today. There are gaps in the data, no allowance was made for depreciation, and no profit-and-loss statement was prepared. Nevertheless, their accounting methods were generally adequate for a 19th-century ironmaster, who was not worried about audits.

For his duties the clerk was paid between $200 and $300 a year, plus room and board, during the 1830s and 1840s. He was also reimbursed for any company travel. Most furnace business, both buying and selling, was conducted on credit. He therefore had to see that drafts were honored by distant banks and that bank notes presented by distant customers were properly discounted. Some payments were delayed or protested, and eventually written off as bad debts, while others took great effort to collect. During these years, the American currency and credit system was undergoing many changes, not all for the best, and a comparatively small business like Hopewell Furnace, which operated with marginal reserves and had a chronic cash-flow problem, often suffered in times of business uncertainty or rapid inflation.

Conditions in the national marketplace could not be predicted, but if an ironmaster kept accurate records, he could control, or at least monitor, his costs, particularly the cost of labor and raw materials. Fortunately, the clerk did not have to prepare a weekly payroll. He merely credited each worker or supplier

The Ironmaster

"Our business is a species of adventure." So wrote an ironmaster in 1850 of a profession in which failure indeed waited for the inept, idle, or unlucky. But in a time of rapidly expanding uses for iron in American industry and transportation, great profits could be made from a charcoal iron furnace if it was guided by a skilled hand. A good ironmaster was a capitalist, technician, market analyst, personnel director, bill collector, purchasing agent, and transportation expert. Many learned the business by working their way up from lower positions at an ironworks. Others, such as Mark Bird, inherited the business and their position from their father. But connections were no guarantee of success. Not everyone could analyze the effects of economic policy in the morning, help the founder correct some deficiency in the furnace in the afternoon, and in the evening play the gracious host to prospective buyers. But for those with the right combination of qualities, wealth, respect, and pride in a good product were the rewards.

Company Clerk

The ironmaster's third hand was the company clerk, a position of prominence on an iron plantation. He kept the books, acted as paymaster, and placated unhappy customers. He also managed the company store, ordering supplies for the village and charging workers' purchases against their wages. He was trusted with setting priorities for filling orders and could extend credit. He also managed the furnace in the ironmaster's absence. The holders of this prestigious job often lived in the home of the ironmaster, a position that an enterprising clerk had a good chance of attaining.

with a dollar amount earned or owed, based on a stated piece or hourly rate. As bookkeeper of the general store, he then charged all purchases or cash advances against this account, maintaining a running balance for each employee or customer. Only a few workers remained consistently in debt on their accounts. Most settled them when they left to seek other employment. Many employees retired or died with a small credit balance, which was often used to pay their funeral expenses. One or two workers were discharged for overdrawing their accounts, and lawsuits were occasionally filed against debtors, but these were exceptions.

The position of clerk often led to a more responsible job as manager of a furnace and sometimes (if he invested his income wisely) as an ironmaster in his own right. Several clerks became ironmasters in the early 1800s, but by mid-century this possibility was becoming increasingly remote, unless one had outside resources or, like John Church, was a relative of an ironmaster. Clement Brooke had little education, but he had both experience and capital, the basic ingredients for success in the 19th century. A few clerks at Hopewell moved into the top managerial ranks. John Benson in 1835 became manager of Oak Grove Furnace in Perry County at a salary of $1,200 per year, and John Church, upon Clement Brooke's death, inherited a half-interest in the Berlin Ironworks in Union County.

Such was Hopewell's management level, simplified yet reasonably efficient for the times. Below the ironmaster and clerk the most important employee was the founder, who was in charge of day-to-day operations at the furnace. He normally worked the day shift, but was on call for serious problems. Assisted by keepers and fillers, he supervised the charging of the furnace with ore, charcoal, and limestone, adjusted the air blast so the furnace would operate at maximum efficiency, and decided when the furnace was ready to tap. When the furnace was "in blast," the founder was a busy man. About every half-hour the stack was charged from the bridge house with 400 to 500 pounds of ore, 15 bushels of charcoal, and 30 to 40 pounds of limestone. To determine the right proportions, he generally relied on his instincts. Scales were not used in the bridge house until 1847.

While the ore was being smelted, the founder kept a close eye on the flames shooting from the top of the stack and the color and separation of the molten iron inside. If the flames were heavy and dark, the furnace was too cold; if bright and smoky, there was too much limestone or not enough ore. The healthiest smelting conditions were indicated by a scarcely visible but lively flame at the top. A good founder spent much of his working time looking into the furnace in order to judge when it was ready to tap. Casting was usually done at 6 in the morning and 6 in the evening. It was signaled by the ringing of the cast house bell, which called the moulders and their helpers to duty. Sometimes a founder also worked as a moulder, thus increasing his income, but his principal responsibility remained the general supervision of furnace operations. He was usually the highest paid worker at the furnace, averaging in the mid-1830s about $600 a year. Instead of an hourly wage he was sometimes paid a stipend based on the tonnage of pig iron and castings produced during each blast.

At least one keeper and two or three fillers assisted the founder, plus several workmen who were variously paid for "putting in the ore," "putting in the night stock," or "stocking coal." When the founder was off duty at night, a keeper supervised operations unless an emergency arose. This was a position held by Clement Brooke early in his career, be-

Furnace Operations

The Founder

The success of an ironmaking operation depended on the experience, skill, and judgement of the founder, whose job it was to keep the furnace running at peak efficiency. A good founder could almost feel what was going on inside the stack. He varied the charge to maintain the proper smelting temperature and determined when the iron was ready to tap. A poor product brought a lower wage and reduced the furnace company's revenue. A poor founder was quickly dismissed.

Fillers

Keeping the furnace charged was one of the hardest and hottest tasks in ironmaking. At the direction of the founder, the fillers dumped barrows and carts of charcoal, ore, and limestone into the "tunnel head." Before scales were used, the founder depended on the fillers to approximate the amount of each ingredient. Fillers had to endure the flame, smoke, and cinders at the tunnel head and work in all weather, but were paid little more than common laborers.

Guttermen

Before the iron was tapped, the guttermen prepared the sand bed on the cast house floor by raking it and digging channels into which the iron flowed. They stacked the hardened bars outside the cast house for transport. Guttermen, often boys, also hauled away the cooling "cinder" to the slag heap.

Furnace Operations

1

3

2

4

Moulders

The casting of iron products was an exacting craft, and the moulders who practiced it were among the highest paid of ironworkers. It took years to gain the necessary skills, and the craft was often passed from father to son. In the early colonial iron casting process, molten iron was run into moulds made by pressing patterns into a sand bed on the cast house floor, or ladled into an open sand mould in a box—"flat-bed" casting. Because the back of a stove plate cast in this method could not be readily angled or curved, the plate was thick and heavy. With the later "flask casting" method, in which both sides of a plate were moulded, it could be lighter and more detailed.

Flask casting was a long and demanding process that required steady hands and great patience. The flask was essentially two open boxes that could be clamped together. A flat, wooden "follow board" was first laid on the moulder's work bench as a base. Then the bottom half of the flask, called the drag, was placed on the follow board, and the wooden pattern placed inside the drag. After dusting the pattern to keep sand from sticking to it, the moulder sifted a fine, damp sand over the pattern with a riddle (1). He then filled the drag to the top with unsifted sand, and packed or "rammed" the sand, first around the edges with the wedge end of the rammer, and then in the center with the broad end (2). The excess sand was then cut away

with the "strike" (3), after which the second follow board was held on the top and the drag turned over. The first follow board was removed, and loose sand was cleaned from the edges with a bellows (4). Now the cope, or top half of the flask, was attached to the drag, and after the other side of the pattern was dusted, more sand was riddled over it. Then a wooden wedge, the "gate," was inserted to form a hole that allowed entry of the molten iron, and sand was rammed around it (5). The excess sand was again cut off with the strike. After the gate was removed, the drag and cope were separated, and the

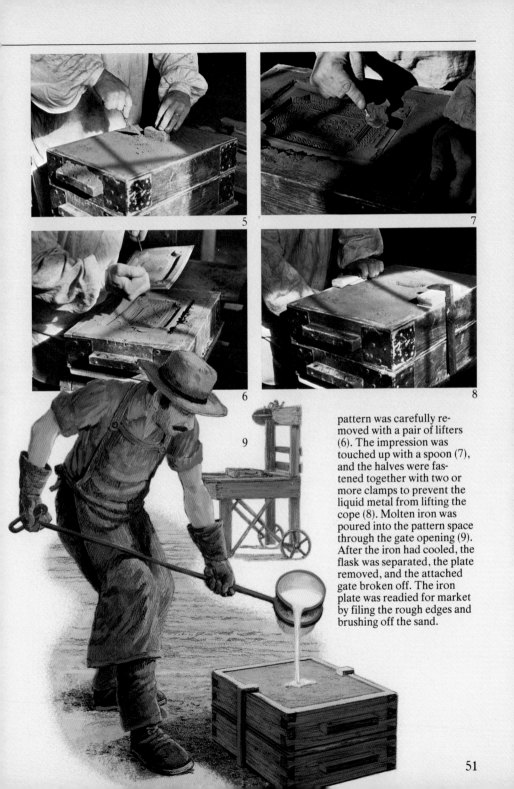

5

7

6

8

9

pattern was carefully re-
moved with a pair of lifters
(6). The impression was
touched up with a spoon (7),
and the halves were fas-
tened together with two or
more clamps to prevent the
liquid metal from lifting the
cope (8). Molten iron was
poured into the pattern space
through the gate opening (9).
After the iron had cooled, the
flask was separated, the plate
removed, and the attached
gate broken off. The iron
plate was readied for market
by filing the rough edges and
brushing off the sand.

fore he became manager. In addition, several guttermen, usually boys, were employed to cart away slag. The fillers were responsible for charging the furnace from the bins or piles of ore, charcoal, and limestone in the bridge house. Because they worked close to the flaming stack opening or tunnel head, their job was hazardous, with a constant risk of burns or other accidents. Fillers were understandably absent more than other workers; the clerk often noted that they were sick or hurt.

The casting arch at the front of the furnace, where the moulders worked, was as hot and dangerous as the tunnel head. These men, the elite of the furnace workers, were paid at a higher rate than the founder. In 1836, they received about $10 a ton for castings, but the founder was sometimes paid for pig iron as well, which boosted his total income. Occasionally a moulder's pay was cut for producing "half-price stoves," defective castings that had to be sold at a reduced price. During the height of the Clement Brooke period, 13 to 19 moulders were employed for each blast, along with 7 to 10 moulder's helpers. Many of these employees left when stove casting was discontinued at Hopewell in 1844. Their skills and the great demand for their services made moulders remarkably independent. They occasionally left without notice when they heard of a better opportunity elsewhere. They were also notorious for taking brief vacations whenever the inclination arose. One day in early September 1825, the clerk reported that 626 pounds of iron had not been cast over the weekend because of "Joseph McKewen, George North and Henry Care Neglecting to mould up . . . as it was their duty to have moulded up. Thomas Care [the father of Henry] told them on Saturday to lade immediately after breakfast and they refused. . . . The Iron all that time was running out of the furnace. McKewen and North was out

hunting with their guns." The three moulders were not punished for their absence, except for the loss of pay for the day, and they all kept their jobs.

The Care family was closely associated with Hopewell for more than 65 years. They gave the furnace three generations of founders and other skilled workers. Thomas Care was a founder from 1818 to 1835, when he was succeeded by his son Henry. Fifteen years later Henry was followed by his son Nathan, who remained until the end of furnace operations in 1883. Thomas and Henry were also trained as moulders, as were three of Thomas's other sons, and therefore the family income was quite high. In 1836 Clement Brooke wrote a glowing letter of recommendation for young John Care, who was seeking employment as a founder at a Maryland furnace. Testifying that "his father Thomas Care has Blowed Hopewell for the last twenty years," Brooke concluded: "I can Safely Recommend John as Capable of Blowing Furnace—is otherwise Sober Moral and upright in his Conduct." The Care family was never wealthy by Brooke standards, but they were always well off and proud of their skills and accomplishments.

Other employees, who worked at a distance from the village, also contributed to the success of the furnace. The 20 or so miners at Hopewell's three mines formed one of these groups of skilled workers. Mining in the early days was a relatively simple occupation. Two men worked as a team in a shallow pit: one man dug the ore and threw it in a bucket or basket, which his partner pulled up by rope and dumped into a wagon. The ore was washed in a sluice to remove the dirt, then hauled to the furnace bank. After the 1830s, much of the ore had to be "roasted" to rid it of sulphur and other impurities before it was delivered to the furnace. As surface deposits were exhausted, mining became more complex, and shafts and tunnels were required to get at the ore. The miners were paid on the weight of the ore delivered to the furnace, although some mining partnerships hired their own workers and operated on a contract basis with the Hopewell management. Judging by furnace records, the miners were comparatively well paid. They averaged more than half the income of the skilled furnace workers, though many worked only part time. The furnace rented some houses to miners, and they had the privilege of shopping at the company store.

Throughout the furnace's history, wood-cutters were the largest group of furnace employees. Of the nearly 250 workers on the payroll from 1835 to 1837, more than 100 were woodcutters. Since most wood-cutting was done in the winter, many of them were part-time employees: neighboring farmers with time on their hands, unemployed boys, and even women hoping to earn a few dollars. According to an estimate in 1830, about 5,000 cords at $1.20 a cord were required to keep the furnace in blast for a year. The furnace was surrounded by hardwood forests of chestnut, oak, hickory, and elm. But the owners were seldom able to cut more than 4,000 cords a year on their own property; they usually had to buy 2,000 to 3,000 more from neighboring wood lots. An acre of forest, depending on the nature and quality of the timber, produced from 30 to 40 cords of wood. (A cord measured 8 feet by 4 feet by 4 feet.) The Hopewell owners practiced clear cutting, leaving the forest to resprout and grow for 30 years before recutting. Woodcutters were paid not only by the cord, but also for the distance from the furnace and the quality of the timber. Distant locations and high-quality timber received a premium, but the price was docked if the cords were stacked over rocks and stumps, piled loosely, or composed of pieces less than 4 feet in length.

After cutting and splitting, the wood was hauled to the coaling areas and made into charcoal. This was done by slowly charring it in "pits" under carefully controlled conditions. These pits, measuring 30 to 40 feet in diameter, were generally located in cleared areas, often near where the wood had been cut. Four-foot lengths of cordwood were stacked on end around a crib-like wooden chimney in the center of the pit. This low mound was then covered with leaves and dirt and set on fire at the center. It took about 25 to 50 cords for each pit. A collier carefully tended the smoldering wood 24 hours a day for 10 to 14 days until it had "come to post" or was completely charred. The coaling process was touchy, for enough heat had to be produced to expel the tar, moisture, and other substances from the wood without consuming the wood itself. Charcoal was only made during spring, summer, and fall.

During the coaling, the master collier and his helpers lived in primitive huts near the pits. A good collier worked as many as eight or nine pits at a time.

Approximately 20 colliers were employed by the furnace throughout the 1830s. A good one produced 35 to 40 bushels of charcoal from each cord of wood. Henry Houck, a productive collier from 1818 to 1842, usually approached this standard. He earned an average annual income throughout this period of over $150. In 1825, one David Hoffman, another exemplary collier, paid the furnace nearly $700 for 2,000 cords of wood, coaled it at a rate of $2.25 per load for a total of 642 loads, and realized a net income for the season of nearly $350.

Fire was the chief hazard facing the collier. Wind could carry sparks from the pit to a nearby stack, an inattentive or sleepy collier or helper could permit the wood to burn too rapidly, or the finished charcoal could be consumed on the way to the charcoal house at the furnace. The last

Feeding the Furnace

Miners

Early miners worked in surface pits, usually in two-man teams. Some were employed by a furnace; others developed mining partnerships and sold ore at contracted prices. By 1806 the Hopewell mineholes required a "screw pump" to remove water.

Woodcutters

A large portion of Hopewell's work force was made up of woodcutters. From 1835 to 1837, 112 out of 213 employees cut wood for charcoal-making. Using only axes, they averaged two cords a day.

1

2

3

Colliers

The long process of making charcoal began when the collier cleared an old hearth (1). In the center he drove a "fagan," a long green pole, around which he built a chimney of small "lapwood" (2). He placed larger "billets"

Teamsters

Furnaces employed their own teamsters or contracted with men who owned teams and wagons. A trip to Philadelphia, for which the furnace paid the teamster's expenses, required several days.

4

6

5

7

against the chimney in two tiers, fitting them together to prevent the pile from "reeling," or twisting (3). He used lapwood to fill in the air spaces (4). To control the burning rate, he covered the pile with leaves and charcoal dust (5). After lighting wood chips in the chimney, the collier could get one night's sleep before constant watching was required. To find "mulls" (soft spots), he had to "jump the pit" — jump up and down on the pile as it burned (6). He dug these mulls out and filled them in to preserve the shape of the pile and maintain even burning. He "coaled out" the finished charcoal slowly (7) to avoid opening drafts which could set the pit aflame.

danger was the most frequent, for colliers in a hurry often failed to allow the charcoal to cool before loading it onto wagons and hauling it to the furnace. The coal sometimes re-ignited on the way, and the wagon could be saved only if the driver stopped, pulled the floorboards from the wagon bed, and scattered the coal on the roadway until the fire was out. Colliers were charged for furnace wood which burned up through neglect. Contracts for coaling usually stated that "the Coal to be drawed a sufficient time before the waggons come so that there be no fire in the Coal." When the charcoal arrived at the furnace, it was stored in the cooling shed until all danger from fire was past, then moved into the capacious charcoal house on the furnace bank.

Among the important semi-skilled workers were the teamsters. Most were independent contractors, but during the furnace's heyday about 10 were regularly on the payroll. They hauled ore from the mines, charcoal from the forests, and limestone from nearby quarries. But most important of all, they carried the finished products to markets far and near, a task which became less time-consuming after the Schuylkill Canal was opened in 1825. Teamsters were paid by the load, plus expenses, meals, lodging, and turnpike and bridge tolls. They also performed services for the less mobile ironmaster and employees, buying goods in the city, paying bills, and occasionally transporting friends and neighbors who were going their way. A teamster's average income was considerably less than a skilled worker's at the furnace. Usually it amounted to less than $100 a year, but David Hart, employed from 1818 to 1840, earned more than $5,000, an average of nearly $475 a year.

A number of artisans also worked at the furnace. One of the most important was the blacksmith, whose shop on the

bank of the creek was a popular gathering place. He made tools for the mine and furnace, occasionally repaired machinery, shod draft animals, forged wagon tires and hardware of all types, and sharpened tools. A wheelwright also labored in his shop to keep the community's vehicles running, and a millwright was occasionally hired when the water wheel or its machinery needed repair. Cabinetmakers, carpenters, masons, and a host of other skilled craftsmen were also employed from time to time as they were needed.

Another important category of labor was farmers and farm workers, some of whom rented farm land from the furnace while others farmed on shares. In 1829 Clement Brooke contracted with farmer Isaac Hayer to "sow thirty acres of winter grain and Sumer grain in proportion . . . and deliver Said Brooke the one half of all the grain in the bushel to Birdsborough Mill and likewise to make and repair all the fences and make all the rails at his own expense." In addition, Hayer agreed to "haul six hundred bushels lime . . . and spread it on the land in a farmer like manner and likewise to find all the clover seed that may be wanted." These farmers, whether employees or tenants, developed the village's arable land and grew much of its food.

Blacks worked at Hopewell throughout its history. Before Pennsylvania abolished slavery in 1780, it is likely that some of Mark Bird's slaves worked at Hopewell. In the early 19th century, southeastern Pennsylvania became a refuge for runaway slaves from Maryland and Virginia. Since Hopewell was only a short distance over the Mason and Dixon Line, some of the blacks employed there probably came from the South. Most held menial jobs and worked irregularly and for only a short time before moving on. Some became longterm employees, however, usually as laborers or teamsters, and a few held semiskilled jobs. William Jacobs, a teamster during most of his career, worked there 60 years, living in the Big House part of that time. Members of the Hill family also had a long-term association with Hopewell Furnace. Wilkinson Hill, a laborer, was first employed in 1827 and remained for 20 years. Benjamin, either his son or his brother, was apprenticed to Clement Brooke and educated at the local school for 4 years at company expense; he then worked as a hostler until his death in 1841. Nine years later Eliza Hill was hired as a maid at the ironmaster's mansion. Moses Morton was a laborer on the furnace bank for 3 years until his three children died in a fire while he and his wife were away from home. Brooke and 25 of his employees contributed to a subscription fund for the bereaved parents who, having lost everything, left the area. Most black workers appear to have been accepted in the community, and many of them or their children were baptized or married in local Episcopal churches. In 1856 several black families established their own church, the A.M.E. Mount Frisby Church, about 3 miles north of the furnace.

Another small but significant element in the labor force were women and children. Despite the characterization by one former employee that Hopewell was "Heaven for horses but Hell for women," many women found employment there, although only a small number were listed as workers on the furnace records. Some of these were seasonal farm laborers, hired during harvest time, while a few worked as miners or woodcutters. In the early 1830s two widows were paid 75¢ a ton for "cleaning castings," the term for removing moulder's sand from stoveplates. Most women, however, found more traditional ways to add to the family income: boarding single men, selling eggs and chickens, marketing home-baked or home-preserved products, and sewing, re-pairing, or laundering clothing. Margaret Benson, the clerk's wife, was paid a weekly wage for 6 years for sewing and "making carpet and quilting for the furnace"; she also made money by selling butter and dried peaches. Other women did sewing and tailoring work for both the company and individual employees during this period. One widow supported herself fully by her expert needlework. Domestic occupations such as these were acceptable in the male-dominated society of mid-19th century America, while female activities at furnace, farm, and forest often became a subject of gossip. One Sarah Hampton, who worked as a woodcutter, was reputed to have had several children out of wedlock. When she and her husband rented a house from the company, it was stipulated that "they must keep a decent and respectable house." The clerk added: "If Sarah's conduct is as it used to be, it will be sufficient at any time to remove them."

Children at Hopewell Furnace, with the possible exception of the Brookes', were not indulged by their parents or guardians. They were expected to take on adult responsibilities as early as possible. Many parents apprenticed their children to masters until they reached the age of 21, or put them to work and collected their wages. Some servants were orphans from the county poorhouse and were bound for a term of years. Others were occasionally apprenticed by widowed mothers living in the vicinity of the furnace. In 1830 Brooke signed an indenture with Sarah Johnston of Union Township, taking on her 5-year-old son David as an apprentice for 16 years. They agreed that the boy "shall not Absent himself day nor night from his said Masters Service without Leave, nor haunt ale-houses, Taverns, or Play houses; but in all things behave himself as a faithfull Apprentice ought to do." In exchange, Brooke agreed to train and educate him and provide food, cloth-

The Furnace Community

Farm

Large acreages were culti-
vated to feed Hopewell's
workers and animals. Two
hundred or more acres of
furnace land were farmed by
tenants who were paid or
sharecropped. The company
also made purchases from local farmers. Hopewell land
produced hay, buckwheat,
rye, corn, wheat, and oats.

Home

Hopewell women performed
the traditional tasks of child-
rearing and homemaking.
Many earned extra income
as teachers, seamstresses,
laundresses, maids, cooks,
and seasonal farm workers.
A few worked as miners or
woodcutters.

School

Children in Hopewell started
school as early as 4 years old,
and continued as long as their
parents could afford to pay
tuition, or until they were old
enough to work. Most of the
teaching was at an elementary level, and parents had to
buy books and writing materials. Tuition teaching lasted
until 1836, when a public
school was opened.

ing, and shelter: "And when he is free to give him one suit of Cloths to be Entirely new and all his old cloths." Young girls were often bound over to work as servants at the Big House until age 18, or to work at furnace-owned farms. Mary Monshour, daughter of a woodcutter, worked out her indenture as a maid and then married the furnace blacksmith, using her "freedom money" and "freedom clothes" as a dowry.

More frequent than the employment of apprentices and indentured servants during this period was the hiring of furnace workers' sons at an early age for a variety of jobs. Boys generally cleaned castings or worked as guttermen in the cast house, hauling cinders to the slag heap, or as fillers, carting ore and charcoal to the tunnel head. Some youths worked as miners or woodcutters with their fathers. Thomas Care, founder, and John Painter, filler, trained their sons to succeed them, and a number of workers' sons learned the moulder's trade at the furnace. In such cases the young person's earnings were credited to his father's or his master's account. Not until they achieved their freedom or reached their majority were these legally dependent young people permitted to keep their own wages. Even after they were grown, many continued to live at home if unmarried, paying for board and laundry.

Small children usually stayed at home and were sternly warned not to play near the furnace, slag pile, blacksmith shop, or creek, or anywhere else that might interfere with work. Since the community was isolated and far from civilizing amenities, the Brookes from the beginning saw the need for a school for the children. A teacher was hired in 1804 to provide elementary education, but the tuition limited students to those from the more substantial families. During the next 25 or 30 years a series of teachers, mostly male, came to Hopewell and held classes in vacant houses or a nearby church. After 1825 school enrollment showed more of a cross-section of the community, as the children of apprentices, blacks, and wood-cutters mingled with the Brooke offspring. The school charged $1.75 a quarter for each pupil, normally beginning in August or September. A second quarter was usually offered in the spring, and a summer session was often available but generally undersubscribed.

In 1834 Pennsylvania enacted a Common School Law, which established a public school system and required its support by State and local taxes. Three years later a one-story stone building, 28 by 38 feet, was constructed with public funds across the creek from the blacksmith shop. This school was large enough to accommodate 25 to 35 pupils seated at long desks lining the walls on three sides. Boys sat on one side and girls on the other, facing the teacher's desk on a raised platform. A stove in the center heated the room. The pupils, ranging in age from 6 to 20, attended school for a 6-month term. The Hopewell school was democratic in spirit and provided a rudimentary education. Disciplinary problems were normally resolved by corporal punishment. Most pupils attended for only 1 to 4 years, ending their formal education at an early age. But the Brooke children and one or two others went on to secondary boarding schools. Education at Hopewell did not appreciably provide a means of upward mobility, but for the fortunate few it did guarantee basic literacy and kept some of the youngsters occupied and in healthy social surroundings for a few years.

Life at Hopewell Furnace was mainly work for everyone, regardless of age, sex, or status. Workers were paid only for the time they worked or for what they produced; there were no holidays or paid vacations. Similarly, no one was laid off unless the furnace was shut down for an extended time, and then everyone suffered, worker and employer alike. The principal difference was that the ironmaster usually had savings he could draw upon, while most workers had little or nothing. Sunday was a day of rest for everyone but furnace workers or colliers. A large part of recreation, therefore, was attending church, which to most 19th-century Americans was as much an emotional as a social or intellectual experience. The Brooke family and a number of workers were communicants of St. Mary's Episcopal Church in nearby Warwick, while others attended Episcopal churches at Douglassville or Morgantown. The church closest to the furnace was Bethesda Baptist Church, less than a mile away, probably built in 1782. During the winter, when travel was often difficult, the Reverend Levi Bull of St. Mary's often came to Hopewell to hold services in private homes or at the schoolhouse.

The main outdoor pursuits were swimming, fishing, hunting, ice-skating, and sleighing. Holidays were times for parties and visiting. The ironmaster held open house on Christmas and New Year's, and the workers and their families were welcome if they were off duty. When the Brookes entertained at the Big House, dancing was popular with all. The end of a blast was traditionally a time for celebration, but Clement Brooke frowned on gambling and drinking. Since drunkenness among workers impaired furnace operations, he banned the sale of whiskey at the company store in 1826 and fined workers for bringing liquor to the job. Brooke and several of his employees subscribed to the *Temperance Advocate*. He was outspoken about temperance, but made no attempt to regulate his workers' lives when they were off duty or away from the furnace property.

To make living and working at the furnace more practical, the management built a number of houses, about 10 to 15 during the Clement Brooke period, and rented them to employees for $12 to $25 a year. Only a few of the houses survive today. They date from the early to mid-19th century, but may be replacements for earlier wooden buildings. Two of the houses are two-story stone structures, with two small rooms downstairs (with a fireplace for heating and cooking) and two small bedrooms upstairs. Since these houses were normally occupied by families of four to eight persons, they were obviously crowded. But furnace records indicate that they were moderately well furnished and had the rudiments of comfort. A larger building, traditionally called the boarding house, lodged some of the single men. Quarters in these buildings were allotted on ability to pay, availability, and the potential tenant's contribution to furnace operations. First priority went to skilled furnace workers.

The company store was operated more for the convenience of the workers than to make a profit. It was managed by the company clerk, who purchased goods and sundries from wholesale merchants in Philadelphia and some supplies from local farmers and millers. The inventory was small and the turnover relatively rapid. Both marketing and billing were informal. The clerk recorded sales on small slips of paper, which were later posted in the day book and journal. He filled special orders for products not in stock, but allowed no discounts for quantity purchases. The average markup from wholesale prices ranged from 15 to 40 percent for most items. Employees could buy goods elsewhere if they had the cash or credit, but Hopewell prices were generally comparable to those charged in other stores in the vicinity. The store's volume was not large, amounting to about $5,000 a year in the early 1830s.

As this account shows, Hopewell Furnace was not run like the stereotype of the late 19th-century factory, with long hours, low wages, and arbitrary rules. On the contrary, most workers at Hopewell regarded themselves, and were so treated, as independent craftsmen who sold their services for an agreed-upon price rather than as laborers who had to accept wages based upon an hourly scale imposed by their employer. This practice was typical of the industrial economy of the United States before the advent of mass production, when machines began to replace skilled workers. An employer like Clement Brooke was respected because he had moved up from the ranks, albeit through family ties, and was therefore knowledgeable about ironmaking. He was treated deferentially by his employees and not regarded as an outsider. In turn, he had a paternalistic concern for his employees, from the lowliest woodcutter to the company clerk. But there were distinctions: in this small society men were valued more according to their function than their social class or income. Hopewell in the 1830s was a community of hardworking individuals who in pursuing their own interests furthered a community enterprise.

Relations between employer and employee at Hopewell reflected this lack of class antagonism. While militant labor organizations were developing among skilled workers in Philadelphia, New York, Baltimore, and other seaboard cities, and strikes and lockouts were on the increase in the 1830s, there was no evident union activity at Hopewell, except for a brief walkout for higher pay at the Jones mine in 1838. Workers were seldom discharged, even for the most flagrant misconduct. If a worker was dissatisfied with his job, he left and usually had little difficulty finding employment elsewhere. The turnover among the less skilled workers was fairly high, but many were migratory workers who could be easily replaced. The stability of the skilled workers, other than the moulders, was remarkable. This can be explained in large part by the ties to the community that many workers developed over generations. In fact, Cares, Painters, Templins, and Houcks—common names on Hopewell's registers—still live in the Union Township, a century after the furnace shut down.

The Tides of Change

Under the redoubtable Clement Brooke, Hopewell Furnace was an efficient, modern operation, able to take advantage of the growing market for iron products. But by mid-century Hopewell was again overtaken by rapid developments in technology. As Brooke was retiring from the iron business, a new industrial era was dawning in America: the age of coal, steam, and steel. The owners of old-fashioned, cold-blast charcoal iron furnaces found it difficult to compete with the coke and hot-blast anthracite furnaces springing up in urban centers to the west. Hopewell made a few attempts to adapt to the new technology, but these only postponed the inevitable. The furnace continued to operate for nearly four more decades, but increasingly it was a technological backwater, struggling to maintain itself against the tides of change.

By the 1850s the United States was entering the take-off stage of economic development. The textile industry was firmly established as the bellwether of American industry, transforming the clothing trades and creating greater demand for factory machinery, machine tools, coal, and iron. The iron industry was second only to textiles in dollar value of manufacturing, though growing demand soon raised it to first place. While the Civil War accelerated industrial development, the real flowering of iron and steel did not come until later. The invention of the Bessemer and open-hearth processes of steel production, the exploitation of soft-coal deposits in western Pennsylvania and adjacent States, the discovery of rich iron ore deposits in the Great Lakes area, and the rapid expansion of railroad networks all combined to render the charcoal-iron industry obsolete.

When Clement Brook retired in 1848, John Church, his wife's nephew, became resident manager. A year later he was supplanted by Dr. Charles M. Clingan, the

Brookes' son-in-law, who was manager for 10 years. The son of an ironmaster, Clingan had received a medical degree in Philadelphia in 1840, but apparently never practiced his profession, preferring business instead. After courting Maria Teresa, the Brookes' eldest daughter, he asked for her hand in a letter to her parents: "In soliciting to become a member of your Family," he wrote, "I have nothing to urge why you should grant the favour; but the kindness and attention you have both invariably treated me with, and the firm attachment I have for your daughter. To support my claims I can neither urge the influence of family conexions, nor the aid of wealth; in lieu of which all I offer is the steady exertion to acquire and support a character which gives me a passport into good society . . ." They were married in 1843. Six years later the Clingans moved into the ironmaster's house.

Clingan was an able manager who developed good relations with his workers, but major decisions were still made by his father-in-law in retirement in nearby Pottstown and the other owners. During his tenure as manager, relations between Clement Brooke and his brother Charles, who held one-third interest in Hopewell Furnace, began to deteriorate. Clingan complained in 1851 that Charles kept putting off paying for pig iron obtained from Hopewell for his Hibernia Forge, and that he absolutely refused to pay interest on the debt. "I tried to reason the matter with him," he said, "but his replies were curses and harsh Epithets such as no Gentleman would use . . . He said to Hell with the interest and that you were a rich man." Clingan concluded: "He is a very unpleasant man to do business with or for—the thing might of been better arranged had Mr. Clement Brooke of been here. He stands in his own light by avoiding Chas. Brooke. I think there is but little prospect of their ever settling their business unless they meet each other face to face." A year after this confrontation the other partners bought out Charles Brooke and reorganized the company. At this time the Hopewell property was worth over $87,800, including nearly 4,000 acres of land.

One likely reason for the disagreement among the partners was Clement Brooke's decision to replace the charcoal furnace with a hot-blast anthracite furnace. This gamble indicated a willingness on his part to change with the times. There were large deposits of anthracite in northeastern Pennsylvania, and the number of furnaces using that fuel had grown rapidly since the late 1830s. The major advantage of iron made with anthracite was greatly reduced labor costs: it was five times cheaper than charcoal iron because no time was spent cutting wood and making charcoal. This more than offset the cost of routing exhaust gas from the top of the stack down to the base to heat the air blast. If this was not reason enough, there were Brooke's successful experience with his anthracite furnace at Robesonia (1845) and his discovery of sulphur ore at Hopewell mine that was unsuitable for the charcoal furnace but which could be used in a hot-blast anthracite furnace.

The new furnace was constructed in 1853 on the hill northwest of the charcoal furnace. It was considerably larger and about 10 feet taller than the original furnace. A new road was also built to the Schuylkill Canal at Monocacy near Birdsboro to transport anthracite coal shipped down from Schuylkill County. Despite expectations, the new furnace was a failure, for in less than 4 years the furnace machinery was moved to Monocacy and installed in a newly built furnace. We can't say for sure why it failed, but the cost of hauling coal from the canal, a distance of 5 miles, was undoubtedly a factor. Moreover, it was found that the high-sulphur ore had to be mixed with other ore to be usable, and such ore was not readily available in quantity. Hopewell's attempt at modernization proved dramatically unsuccessful, and the owners decided to go back to traditional methods of production.

Shortly after this setback, Clement Brooke moved to Philadelphia, and after a time was joined there by his daughter and her family. Dr. Clingan departed soon after. He entered the banking and the grocery business in the city, but returned to Hopewell frequently to look after his interests, especially after Brooke's death 2 years later. Although Mrs. Clingan inherited her father's share of the property, under the laws of the time her husband controlled her wealth during his lifetime. After 1861 the Hopewell firm was known as Clingan and Buckley. John R. Shafer, the furnace clerk, became the resident manager, a position he held for about 15 years. Throughout the waning two decades of furnace activities neither of the partners took an active part in its day-to-day operations. Clingan died in 1875 with an estate valued at nearly $27,500, of which $10,000 was his share of the Hopewell property. After his death his widow and her partner Edward S. Buckley appointed Harker Long, Shafer's successor as clerk, manager of the furnace, a position he held until it closed down.

The Civil War temporarily revived Hopewell and other surviving charcoal iron furnaces. The price of pig iron rose from about $30 a ton before the war to $80 to $100 at the end. Railroad expansion kept demand high after the war. This upsurge in business encouraged extensive repairs of the furnace complex in 1869. The next year A. Whitney and Sons, a Philadelphia manufacturer of railroad car wheels, contracted to buy most of Hopewell's production for the next decade, and in 1876 the Reading Railroad Company began buying iron from the furnace.

Nathan Care was Hopewell's founder from 1850 until the final blast in 1883. The founder position had been held by his father and grandfather continuously since 1819. Care attended school at Hopewell, and worked as a moulder and keeper before becoming founder. From 1859 to 1861 he was also hired manager of the furnace. Care employed his son as his keeper, or assistant, and received payment from the furnace for boarding him. His son, also named Nathan, managed the Hopewell property from 1916 to 1935, living in the rear wing of the ironmaster's mansion.

The 1870s, however, were not prosperous for Hopewell. Optimism soon gave way under the impact of the business panic of 1873. The furnace was out of blast in 1874 and again in 1877-78, but the rise in the price of iron at the end of the decade encouraged the owner to resume operations in 1880. Buckley ordered Long early that year to "Get all the wood cut off the property that it is possible to get out by paying as much wages as any one else in the neighborhood; and blow the furnace *as early in the Spring as it may be possible to get coal made from our own wood* . . . and keep her going until all our own coal is consumed and then blow out." After a successful blast, the severe winter of 1881 forced the furnace to close down again. The water wheel froze up at one point, cutting off the air blast. A local newspaper reported that because of the cold "the proprietors of Joanna and Hopewell Furnaces have been unable to get their usual quantity of wood cut for burning charcoal for these establishments, and fears are entertained that they will have to close their works . . . for want of fuel." To avoid a crippling loss of power again, a boiler was installed, heated by hot gases from the furnace stack, to run an auxiliary steam engine.

In 1882 an ore roaster was constructed next to the furnace to remove impurities from the ore before smelting, and the water wheel and blast machinery were substantially rebuilt. Buckley opposed spending money for these improvements. His prediction that "Hopewell is about 'played out' and next years blast is probably the last she will ever make" proved to be true. The final blast at Hopewell came to an end on June 15, 1883, and the furnace was shut down permanently.

During the ensuing 5 years the pig iron, ore, and wood on hand were gradually sold off and the furnace account books closed out. Harker Long remained as caretaker until 1896. For some years the property continued to produce an income. Fence posts and rails were cut and sold in carload lots, customers were found for the charcoal that continued to be produced, and stone quarrying rights were sold to a local company. Until 1913 the Pottstown Iron Company mined ore on lease from the old Hopewell mine. All through these years Buckley, who tired of paying taxes and spending money for repairs, tried to sell the property. In 1894 he finally swapped his interest in the furnace to Mrs. Clingan for property she owned in Philadelphia.

Hopewell's decline was fairly predictable after the 1840s. As it was, the furnace was one of a dwindling number that survived into the 1880s. By this time the center of the American iron and steel industry had moved west to the Pittsburgh area and south to Birmingham, Alabama, closer to large deposits of bituminous coal and newly discovered mountains of iron ore. The formerly virgin landscape in those areas was now dotted with coking ovens, blast furnaces, rolling mills, and Bessemer converters or open-hearth steel furnaces. Young Andrew Carnegie made Pittsburgh his headquarters. Within a few decades he developed the most important and efficient iron and steel complex in the United States. Like other industrialists of the Gilded Age, he quickly saw the virtues of combining all processes in the manufacture of steel, from raw materials to the finished product, under control of one company, absorbing many of his competitors along the way. Given the rapid integration of the iron and steel industry during the last decades of the 19th century, it is surprising that Hopewell Furnace survived as long as it did. Nevertheless, Hopewell and its fellow charcoal-iron furnaces laid the groundwork for the development of the United States as a major industrial power. This was their significance in American history.

During the last decades of Hopewell's operation, it was one of a dwindling number of cold-blast furnaces still trying to compete with heavily capitalized Bessemer and open-hearth steel operations. After stove plate casting was abandoned at Hopewell in 1844, the growing demand for pig iron kept the furnace in operation. A brief revival was sparked by the Civil War, which tripled the price of iron, but that only postponed the inevitable. Despite extensive repairs and renewed activity after the war in response to high iron prices and the demand for charcoal iron for railroad car wheels, the furnace was out of blast for 2 to 3 years during the 1870s. Attempts at modernization, including an anthracite furnace in 1853, a steam engine in 1880, and an ore roaster in 1882 (at right in top photo) did not halt the decline. After the final blast in 1883, the property remained productive. Wood was still sold for fence posts and railroad ties. Stone was quarried, farming continued, and there was a brief renewal of charcoal making in 1902 for Philadelphia iron manufacturers. The ironmaster's mansion served as the caretaker's quarters and as a summer home for the owners. Hopewell also remained a gathering place for area farmers. The early 1890s photo at bottom left shows what is perhaps an auction. The cast house rapidly fell into decay, as shown in the 1887 photo at top. Books were kept until 1896, the year of the photo at bottom right. When the Federal Government bought the property from Mrs. Louise Brooke in 1935, descendents of Hopewell Furnace workers still lived in the tenant houses.

Hopewell Restored

At the turn of the century Hopewell Furnace had the aspect of a deserted village. Many buildings were badly deteriorated. Even the massive stone furnace was slowly falling apart, and the forest was beginning to reclaim the site, obscuring its industrial origins. The owners of the property at this time were the children of Charles and Maria Clingan: Louise Clingan Brooke and her two brothers. They still shared an attachment to the ancestral home and with their families continued to travel out from Philadelphia to spend summers there. In 1930, nearly 50 years after the last blast, scholars from Philadelphia's Franklin Institute visited the site to see what of historical value still remained. When they expressed interest in the decaying water wheel and blast machinery, Mrs. Brooke offered it to them, and the machinery was dismantled and stored pending its removal to the institute. At this point the Federal Government became interested in the area, not because of its historical significance but for its use in the New Deal conservation program. In 1935 the government paid Mrs. Brooke nearly $100,000 for more than 4,000 acres, acquiring about 1,500 acres from other owners. That year two Civilian Conservation Corps camps were established in the area. Trails were built through woods, French Creek was dammed to create Hopewell Lake, and campsites and picnic areas constructed. Government planners saw this virtually deserted tract of land as a useful "park and pleasuring ground" for the growing population of southeastern Pennsylvania.

Shortly after obtaining title to the property, the U.S. Department of the Interior sent National Park Service historian Roy E. Appleman to survey the site's history. Impressed by the ruins, Appleman began to seek out documents and interview former inhabitants of the area, including Harker Long, still alert at 85. Appleman urged the restoration of the old ironmaking

complex. Admitting that "it is from Mr. Long that we have obtained practically all the information in this report portraying Hopewell of an earlier day," he recommended that "a restoration might be undertaken . . . (which) would be to a high degree accurate and reliable in its historical and cultural details."

On the basis of Appleman's recommendations the Works Progress Administration, using CCC labor, began a systematic investigation of the area. Further interviews were conducted, research was pursued in State and county archives, and archeological excavations were undertaken, especially in the furnace area. Meantime, the Franklin Institute deeded its interest in the water wheel and blast machinery to the government. CCC workers stabilized the old furnace, cleaned out the wheel pit and races, and recorded the other buildings. Other than the furnace group, the buildings still standing in reasonably good condition were the ironmaster's house, the office and store, the spring house, the blacksmith shop, and four tenant houses.

The assumption that Hopewell's furnace and system of water had changed little from colonial times to the end of its operations in the late 19th century provided the basis of the first restoration plan. But interviews with former residents and extensive research indicated that Hopewell throughout its long history had been a constantly changing community and that the period with the least documentation was the 18th century. The furnace could not therefore be restored to the era of the American Revolution, and there was little enthusiasm for restoring the community to the years of decline after the Civil War. As research proceeded, it became obvious that Hopewell should portray its most prosperous and productive time, the period between 1820 and 1840, when it was typical of an important

(Top) 1925 photo of Hopewell's last waterwheel and blast machinery. In 1881 a steam engine was installed for auxiliary power. (Bottom) Civilian Conservation Corps team prepares timber for stabilizing ruined furnace stack in 1936.

stage in the evolution of the American iron industry.

In 1938 the Secretary of the Interior designated the area as a National Historic Site within the National Park System. World War II interrupted further research and development, but in 1946 the Federal Government decided to separate the historic and recreational areas in the tract. More than 5,300 acres, including the Hopewell Lake recreational area, were deeded to the Commonwealth of Pennsylvania, reducing the historic site to 848 acres.

Much historical, architectural, and archeological research has been done since that time, and a good deal of physical restoration and reconstruction based on those investigations. After the furnace, the next major restoration was the blacksmith shop. During WPA days, it was again a vital operation in the community, manned constantly and providing tools for many activities.

Old furnace records were explored for clues to furnace operations, and photographs from the post-Civil War period were analyzed for information on the physical changes in the community. Architects and archeologists ferreted out secrets which the documentary evidence did not provide. Minor structures such as the bake ovens and spring house were investigated and restored, and research was undertaken on the tenant houses and buildings outside of the immediate community. The most intensive investigation centered on the furnace group. After several archeological studies in this area, sufficient data were finally obtained to reconstruct these buildings accurately. Other buildings were restored to their period of significance, and the historic roads were re-established as foot trails for visitors.

The water wheel and blast machinery proved to be one of the greatest challenges for restorers. Both were so badly deteriorated that they had to be completely rebuilt. Timbers were cut, shaped, adzed, and treated with creosote. The leather in the piston tubs, the hickory rings, and the metal springs were replaced, and the wheel pit and supporting timbers were reconstructed. To bring water to the wheel, the west head race was rebuilt, and in 1952 the new water wheel was put back in operation.

Hopewell today depicts the industrial community that flourished here in the early 19th century. During the summer, moulding and metal casting, blacksmithing, and other traditional skills are demonstrated. Livestock graze in the meadows, and the water wheel and blast machinery toil away. But even with this pageantry, an important ingredient is missing from the scene and must be supplied by the visitor's imagination. The atmosphere at the site today is more nostalgic than realistic. The dirt, the sweat, the occasional suffering are absent. Life was uncompromising here in the 19th century. Yet it was generally satisfying and productive, and the contribution of each worker, from woodcutter to manager, was respected, creating a feeling of community. It is difficult now to recapture this feeling, but it was real in the 19th century and it contributed to the community's well being. Hopewell was more than an accumulation of picturesque structures; it was a place vibrant with life, but of a kind foreign to most Americans today. Yet for all the impossibility of recovering the vanished substance of the past, this reconstructed iron plantation can help us understand how the American industrial economy of today developed—with its problems as well as its continuing promise.

– Walter Hugins

Recapturing the Past

Neglect and the elements had taken their toll by the time the Federal Government bought the Hopewell property in 1935 from Mrs. Louise Clingan Brooke, whose family had owned the property for 135 years. The furnace stack, "Big House," spring house, office store, four tenant houses, blacksmith shop, and several other structures were still standing. The 5,198-acre property became a Recreation Demonstration area administered by the Works Progress Administration, using the labor of 400 men in Civilian Conservation Corps (CCC) camps. At the time the land was purchased, the historic significance of Hopewell Furnace wasn't realized. Largely due to the efforts of historian Roy Appleman, whose 1935 report strongly recommended restoration, the National Historic Site was established in 1938. The furnace was restored and the other structures were stabilized. World War II ended the CCC project, and the CCC camp became a rest area for British and French sailors. In 1947 most of the property with the recreation facilities was deeded to the Commonwealth of Pennsylvania, leaving 848 acres in the historic site. Restoration began in earnest in the 1950s, with emphasis on the 1820-40 period. By 1952 the blast machinery had been rebuilt and put into operation. The barn, cooling shed-connecting shed, tenant houses, and cast house were restored. The cast house is different from the one shown in the 1887 photograph on page 67, due to several modifications before the final blast. Here, as in all the buildings, 19th century construction methods, such as wooden dowels to join the handhewn beams, were used.

Part 3

Guide to Hopewell

Visiting The Park

Hopewell Furnace is a window on industrial life as it was a century and a half ago. While hundreds of blast furnaces in varying states of ruin and preservation remain throughout the eastern United States, Hopewell is the most completely restored ironmaking community. Brought back to its appearance in 1820-40 by the National Park Service, it represents the many such ironworks that thrived in America's industrial youth. While the present-day site is cleaner, quieter, and greener than when the furnace was "in blast," with a little imagination visitors will find themselves in the midst of a busy iron plantation whose rhythms were tuned to the operation of the furnace. During the summer the interpretive program presents such activities as charcoal-making and moulding. Hopewell is not a place to rush through. Take your time. Listen to the low rushing of the air blast in the furnace. Notice the varied architecture. You'll witness a way of life that endured for more than 150 years; you'll recognize the roots of an industry vital to the nation's growth.

At the visitor center, exhibits, illustrated programs, and examples of cast iron products provide a good introduction to the site. On the following pages, the panoramic view of the site and accompanying text will acquaint you with the history behind the structures.

Hopewell Furnace is located about 5 miles south of Birdsboro on Pa. 345. It is 10 miles from the Morgantown interchange on the Pa. Turnpike, via Pa. 23 East and 345 North. Address inquiries to: Superintendent, Hopewell Furnace National Historic Site, R.D. 1. Elverson, PA 19520. (215) 582-8773.

1 Over the **Village Roads**, supplies and raw materials necessary to sustain the furnace and village were brought in. Furnace products were shipped to market on these same roads. Hopewell was built near the 1757 Coventry Forge-Reading road. Private roads connected the furnace with the 1757 road and Hopewell Mine. Other public roads vital to Hopewell were built in 1772, 1804, 1815, 1827, and 1856. These dirt roads were often impassable and were repaired with slag by furnace employees.

3 At the **Charcoal Hearths**, scattered around Hopewell's forest lands, 5,000 to 6,000 cords of wood a year were "coaled" to produce charcoal fuel. Colliers lived in earth and log **Collier Huts** near the "pits," where cordwood was stacked around a chimney to form a cone-shaped mound. After firing the mound, the colliers continuously monitored its burning rate for 10 to 16 days. A good yield was 35 to 40 bushels per cord. The **Charcoal Kilns** were built in the 1850s but had limited success.

4 The **Charcoal House** and **Cooling Shed** kept the charcoal fuel dry. The charcoal house could hold 90,000 bushels. The charcoal brought by wagons from the hearths was sometimes still smouldering. Teamsters were known to drive their wagons into streams to put out fires. When wagons arrived at the cooling shed, the floorboards were pulled out to dump the charcoal. It was then thoroughly checked for hot coals before being shoveled into the charcoal house.

2 The **Anthracite Furnace,** in production by 1853, was an attempt to modernize Hopewell's operation. The anthracite furnace complex included a cast house, a storage house for coal, a heating furnace, and a bridgehouse to the furnace top. An engine house contained a steam engine and blower to force the heated blast into the three tuyeres. High shipping costs for the anthracite, poor quality ore, and possible structural defects contributed to its failure around 1855.

5 The **Furnace Bank**—a dugout hill with a retaining wall— was a standard feature of early charcoal furnaces. Charcoal, limestone, and ore from the bank were moved in carts along the **Connecting Shed** to the **Bridgehouse** at the top of the furnace. Under the direction of the founder, the fillers "charged" the furnace with measured amounts of raw materials (averaging 15 bushels of charcoal, 400 to 500 pounds of iron ore, and 30 to 40 pounds of limestone) every half hour.

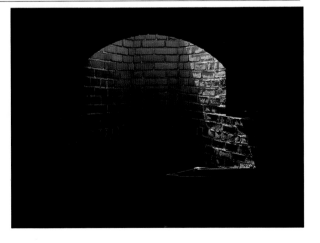

6 The **Water Wheel,** turned by water carried by the **East and West Headraces,** drove the furnace's **Blast Machinery.** Eighteenth century furnaces used two huge bellows operated by a camshaft off the waterwheel. Hopewell's original 30-foot wheel powered this type of apparatus and was oriented on a north-south axis. About 1805 a 22-foot wheel was constructed along an east-west axis. In the present system, in operation by 1822, the wheel moves two piston rods alternately to compress air in the wooden "blowing tubs." The compressed air moves into the receiving box between the tubs, and then through a long pipe to enter the furnace through the tuyere, a cone-shaped copper nozzle attached to the pipe. Pressure was about three-quarters of a pound per square inch.

7 The **Hopewell Store,** operating by 1784, was the nearest source of basic goods for most furnace workers. Money rarely changed hands; employees received credit for their work on the company books and were debited by the clerk for store purchases. Some villagers bartered dairy products, vegetables, and poultry. Dry goods, foodstuffs, tools, agricultural implements, tobacco, and salt were commonly stocked, along with iron products of the furnace. Luxury items such as coffee, chocolate, and ready-made clothing were usually available. Such things as watches could be ordered from the city. Hopewell workers were not required to buy at the store, but prices were competitive, and the store was convenient. One corner of the store served as the clerk's office.

8 In the **Cast House** molten iron was cast into stove plates, pots, and many other products. In early casting, molten iron was poured into impressions made in sand. By the late 18th century, moulders were using the more efficient "flask casting" method. (See pg. 50.) As many as 8 moulders worked each 12-hour shift preparing moulds and casting when the furnace was tapped. To prevent fire from furnace cinders, the roof was covered with handmade tiles that were grooved to channel rainwater. The **Ore Roaster** (now gone), located next to the cast house, was built in 1882 to remove such impurities as sulphur from iron ore. After being heated to a "cherry red" in the 12-foot, iron-plated roaster, the ore was removed from the base.

9 When the **Furnace** was erected around 1771, it was a typical, charcoal-fueled, cold-blast furnace. When it went out of blast in 1883, it had been obsolete for more than 30 years. The furnace stack is $32\frac{1}{2}$ feet high. The interior is 7 feet wide at the bosh (the widest point), tapering to $1\frac{1}{2}$ feet at the top, or "tunnel head." The outside wall is built of fieldstone. The interior, or "inwall," was lined with refractory sandstone. Molten iron and slag dripped down to the bottom of the furnace. The slag, floating on the iron, was drawn off through the "cinder notch." The iron was "drawn out" from a hole at the bottom of the dam stone every 12 hours. Heat, chemical reactions, and friction wore away the inwalls and hearth until the furnace had to go "out of blast" about once a year for repairs.

84

10 At the **Cleaning Shed** castings were cleaned before being shipped to customers. Cooled castings were moved from the cast house to the cleaning shed, where sand was brushed from the casting and rough edges filed off. The clerk checked for defective plates, for which moulders received half pay as "gate metal." Moulders cleaned their own castings or paid others to do the work, including women and children. In 1832, moulders paid 75 cents per ton for cleaning.

⓫ The **Blacksmith Shop** (1775?) is one of the oldest structures in the village. Rising water levels and slag deposition outside the shop resulted in the walls and forge being raised twice by 1849. The furnace blacksmith made wagon wheel tires and tools for farm, mine, and furnace. He repaired machinery for the furnace and neighboring farmers; shod mules, horses, and oxen; made hardware items such as hinges, latches, bolts, locks, and lock plates; sharpened harrow teeth and hoes; and steeled axes.

⓭ **Tenant Houses** were built by the furnace company to maintain a readily available workforce. In 1855 the furnace was taxed for 14 tenant houses. Houses were also built at the "mineholes" for Hopewell miners. Many workers lived off furnace property in their own houses. For those who lived in the 2- or 4-room company houses, rent was $12 to $25 a year. Tenants were often allowed to gather "old decayed timber" for firewood from furnace lands. The southernmost of the tenant houses is a duplex. More windows, a full attic, a basement, and a small barn indicate that the house was probably built for someone of importance at the furnace. The first occupant may have been John Church, nephew of Mrs. Clement Brooke and clerk at Hopewell in 1845. The **Boarding House** may date to 1806; it was enlarged in 1830. The furnace paid tenant house residents for boarding workers. The boarders were single men and sometimes family members. Traditionally, the "boarding house" was used for that purpose.

⓬ The **Schoolhouse** was built in 1837 by the furnace company, which was reimbursed by the school district. As early as 1807 education was provided through subscription from families with school age children. Pupils came from all economic levels, though children from higher-income families predominated. As many as 27 pupils, black and white, sat in the single 28- by 33-foot building, with boys on the north side, girls on the south. One "led pencell" cost a pupil's family 12½ cents, half a day's pay for farm work.

⑭ The **Barn,** enlarged several times, reached its present size by about 1840. The draft animals sheltered here were crucial to Hopewell's operation. The lower barn contained stalls for 36 horses or mules. Above the stalls were three hay mows which held enough hay to feed the animals for a year. Feed grain was stored in bins at opposite ends of the barn. Today the barn houses a variety of period horse-drawn wagons, carriages, and sleighs.

⑮ In the **Spring House,** perishables were kept in crocks submerged in the cold spring water that flowed in a trough through the building. In the southern washroom water was heated in large iron kettles for washing clothes. The room was also used for rendering lard, making soap and candles, and cooking apple butter. The northern spring room supplied drinking water for the Big House and for furnace workers. The loft provided storage for furniture, jars, and dishes, and held drying herbs and grains.

⑯ In the **Smoke House** meat was hung over a fire of green wood or corncobs, which filled the building with smoke for several days until the meat absorbed the flavor. Smoking also firmed and dried the meat, preventing spoilage. The **Bake Oven** produced bread and pastries and was used to dry fruit and corn. Meals were prepared in the **Moulders Kitchen** for the moulders, who ate in the **Dining Room** in the Big House basement. The moulders needed to be near the furnace when it was tapped.

Hopewell's Wagons and Carriages

2-Wheel Dump Cart

Freight Wagon

Charcoal Wagon

One-Horse Chaise

17 The **Ironmaster's Mansion** at Hopewell, although large and well-appointed, was modest compared to many. This house was built in three stages between 1800 and 1828. The 4-story, 19-room, T-shaped mansion, called the "Big House," accommodated the ironmaster, his family, and usually servants who had living quarters on the fourth floor. Guests and traveling businessmen stayed overnight in one of the third floor rooms. Business transactions were conducted in the second floor study, which also served as a library and sitting room. The second-floor parlor is furnished in early Victorian style, reflecting the tastes of ironmaster Dr. Charles Clingan and his family. The melodeon, which belonged to Maria Brooke, was common in affluent households of the day. Played by the ladies, it provided entertainment before and after dinner. The dining room retains its original architectural detail, window trim, and mantelpiece from the early 19th century. Meals were prepared in the second-floor kitchen.

18 The **East Headrace** ran from Baptism Creek to the water wheel. The race passed under the village road through an iron pipe, and then ran to the waterwheel. Above the headrace the terraced **Ironmaster's Garden** contained a grape arbor, apiary, and a summerhouse. Pavilions, paths, and rows of boxwood separated beds of roses, poppies, violets, and other flowers. Asparagus, herbs, and strawberries complemented the flower garden. A full-time gardener cared for the gardens and 1829 greenhouse.

90

Bethesda Church (1782?) was the place of worship for many Hopewell employees. A Baptist congregation was formed in 1827, and a nearby stream was known as Baptizing Creek. The tombstones serve as a partial record of Hopewell employees. The earliest marked tombstone is that of Thomas Kirby, a woodcutter, dated May 10, 1807. Andrew Collins, an early minister, also acted as schoolmaster for Hopewell's children. See map, page 94, for location of church, which is still used on Sundays.

Living History at Hopewell

Although the furnace can never be fired up for another "campaign," Hopewell is alive in summer with demonstrations, by people in period dress, of the tasks associated with the furnace operation of a representative 19th-century ironmaking community. The ring of the blacksmith's hammer can be heard throughout the village. In the tenant houses people go about the chores of gardening, cooking, weaving, candlemaking, and

soapmaking. The furnace clerk explains bookkeeping and minds the store that served Hopewell's inhabitants. Near the furnace a col- lier performs the hard and dirty work of turning wood into the charcoal that fed the insatiable furnace. One can see in the cast house the proc- ess toward which all the other activities in the village were directed—the moulding and casting of liquid metal into finished products.

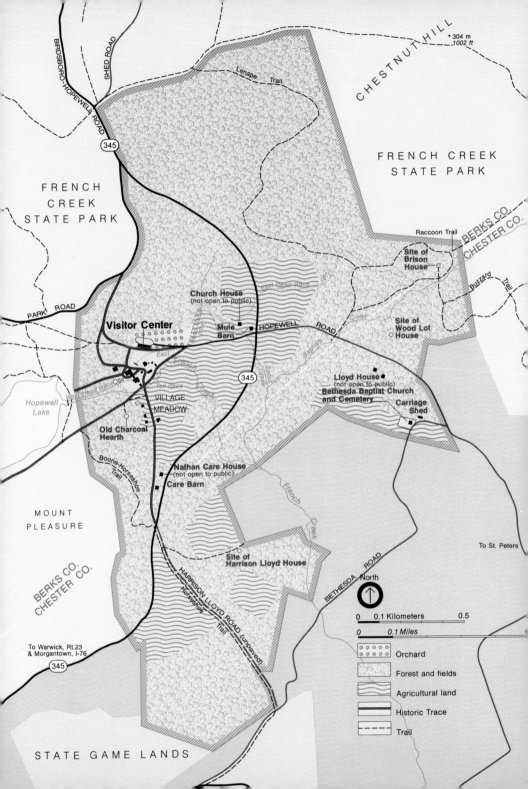

The following sites preserve other vestiges of the early iron industry. At some sites only the furnace stack remains; others have been largely restored. The site administrator should be contacted for information on hours and facilities.

Alabama

Tannehill Ironworks (1830)
Tannehill Historical
State Park
Route 1, Box 124
McCalla, AL 35111

Sloss Furnaces (1927)
P.O. Box 11781
3105 1st Ave., North
Birmingham, AL 35202

Maine

Katahdin Ironworks (1843)
Maine Bureau of Parks
Katahdin Ironworks Road
Brownville, ME 04414

Maryland

Catoctin Furnace (1774)
Cunningham Falls State Park
Thurmont, MD 21788

Lonaconing Iron Furnace (1836)
Allegany County Historical
Society
218 Washington Street
Cumberland, MD 21502

Nassawango Furnace (1832)
Furnace Town, Inc.
P.O. Box 207
Snow Hill, MD 21863

Massachusetts

Saugus Ironworks (1646)
Saugus Ironworks National
Historic Site
244 Central Street
Saugus, MA 01906

Michigan

Fayette Furnace (1867)
Fayette State Historic Park
13700 13.25 Lane
Garden, MI 49835

Missouri

Maramec Ironworks (1826)
Maramec Museum
P.O. Box 305
St. James, MO 65559

New Jersey

Batsto Village (1766)
Wharton State Forest
R.D. #4
Hammonton, NJ 08037

Howell Works (1790)
Allaire State Park
Allaire, NJ 07727

Ringwood Ironworks (1742)
Ringwood State Park
Box 1304, Sloatsburg Road
Ringwood, NJ 07456

Ohio

Buckeye Furnace (1851)
Buckeye Furnace State
Memorial
123 Buckeye Park Road
Wellston, OH 45692

Pennsylvania

Caledonia Furnace (1837)
Caledonia State Park
40 Rocky Mountain Road
Fayetteville, PA 17222

Cornwall Furnace (1742)
P.O. Box 251
Cornwall, PA 17016

Eagle Furnace (1810)
Roland Curtin Foundation
R.D. #3, Box 88
Howard, PA 16841

Greenwood Furnace (1837)
Greenwood Furnace
State Park
R.D. #2
Huntingdon, PA 16652

Hibernia Furnace (1793)
Chester County Parks
235 West Market Street
West Chester, PA 19380

Joanna Furnace (1792)
Hay Creek Valley Historical
Association
Box 36
Geigertown, PA 19523

Lock Ridge Furnace (1868)
Lock Ridge Furnace Museum
Franklin Street
Alburtis, PA 19464

Pine Grove Furnace (1764)
Pine Grove Furnace
State Park
R.D. #2
Gardners, PA 17324

Scranton Furnaces (1841)
R.D. #1, Bald Mountain Road
Scranton, PA 18504

Saugus Ironworks

Maramec Ironworks

Greenwood Furnace

Handbook 124

Sources and Readings
The most complete history of Hopewell Furnace,
based upon extensive research in surviving records,
is Joseph E. Walker, *Hopewell Village: A Social and
Economic History of an Ironmaking Community*
(Philadelphia, 1966); this account is indebted to
Walker's study. A pioneering history of the colonial
period is Arthur C. Bining, *Pennsylvania Iron Manufacture in the 18th Century* (Harrisburg, 1938). For
details on the physical development of Hopewell Furnace, students should consult the 50 or more archeological, historical, and architectural research reports
sponsored by the Park Service. Nearly every building and structure has been the subject of thorough
investigation.

Among the older but still useful accounts are
Frederick Overman, *The Manufacture of Iron* (Phila-
delphia, 1850); John B. Pearse, *A Concise History
of the Iron Manufacture of the American Colonies
up to the Revolution and of Pennsylvania until the
Present Time* (Philadelphia, 1876); and J.P. Lesley,
*The Iron Manufacturer's Guide to the Furnaces,
Forges, and Rolling Mills of the United States* (New
York, 1859). Alfred Gemmell, *The Charcoal Iron
Industry in the Perkiomen Valley* (Morristown, 1949)
is an interesting regional study. Henry C. Mercer,
The Bible in Iron (Doylestown, 1914) is a well-illus-
trated study of early stoveplate casting.

Several general works provide a useful perspective
on Hopewell Furnace. See, for example, William A.
Sullivan, *The Industrial Worker in Pennsylvania,
1800-1840* (Harrisburg, 1955); W. Paul Strassman,
*Risk and Technological Innovation: American Manu-
facturing Methods during the 19th Century* (Ithaca,
1959); and George Rogers Taylor, *The Transportation Revolution, 1815-1860* (New York, 1951).